6-10-23

SURVIVOR

SURVIVOR

A STORY OF TRAGEDY, GUILT, *and* GRACE

DUANE C. MILLER

Discovery House.
from Our Daily Bread Ministries

To the memory of Don Enzor, Chuck Schnittker, and Tim Meadows.
Your love for Jesus and your total surrender to Him
is a legacy that is still transforming lives around the world.
What an example you left for us to follow!

CONTENTS

PERSPECTIVE FROM
THE BOTTOM OF THE LAKE

I had never known such excruciating pain.

I was far beyond exhaustion, and every muscle in my body had cramped. My lungs, full of water, felt as though daggers had been plunged into them.

Again and again, I fought and clawed my way to the surface of Opeongo Lake. Breaking through the surface, I grabbed the side of the swamped canoe and pulled myself up and across the top of it, struggling to breathe. Almost instantly, the canoe rolled like a barrel beneath me again—plunging me back under the surface before I could catch my breath. I was still inhaling as I sunk back under the surface—so instead of breathing in air, I sucked in more water.

Even though I was young, a good swimmer, and in good physical condition, I was totally spent. Time and time again I struggled back to the surface gasping for air, only to be pulled under again. There was not one ounce of strength left in me, but I was not going to give up. Frantically, I fought for my life because dying was not an option!

Suddenly, a calm swept over me, and I began to relax. The struggle had ended. I stopped trying to swim to the surface, and I allowed myself to sink into the depths of the lake. Lying back in the water, all

exhaustion and pain began to fade away, and I found myself thinking, *Wow, is this what it is like to die? Okay Lord, I am ready to meet you,
so here I come.* An indescribable feeling enveloped me. The fear and
terror I once felt disappeared, and my struggle to stay alive faded as
peace washed over me.

Just as I accepted my fate, I heard the Lord speak to my heart with
a kind but authoritative voice, "I'm not through with you yet, Miller,
so get back up there!" Suddenly, my muscles relaxed and uncramped,
and I felt Him give me the strength to swim to the surface one more
time. It was as if someone had grabbed me by the scruff of the neck
and pulled me up. Exhaustion and pain disappeared as a surge of
energy shot through my body. I looked up at the underside of the
canoe and kicked and swam my way toward it.

I broke through the surface and clutched the side of the swamped
canoe. This time it didn't roll. Al DesChamps, one of my canoeing
partners, was hanging onto the other side of the canoe—counterbal-
ancing it for me. Locking my armpits over the gunnels of the canoe,
I coughed out the water in my lungs and breathed deeply.

I looked around. As I did, I realized that three of us were missing.
Where were Don, Chuck, and Tim?

CHAPTER ONE

MAN OF THE STAR

The sweat was still dripping off my chin as I stood with my hands on my hips, catching my breath, when Chuck's feet hit the ground after climbing the ten-foot cargo rope at the end of the obstacle course.

"I can't believe that buzzard did it to me again!" I exclaimed as Howie Reinhold showed me the time on the stopwatch. My cousin Chuck Schnittker had just beaten my record on the military obstacle course at Trail to Life Camp (TTLC). Twice that week I had owned the record, only to have Chuck break it and reclaim bragging rights.

As long as I could remember, Chuck and I had competed in everything—whether it was foot races, cherry pit spitting, or seeing who could skip a stone the farthest. Bragging rights meant everything to us.

The obstacle course was just one thing that made the TTLC programs unique among Christian camps. From the moment the young people entered the mess hall to register, they were "privates" in a military-style boot camp—and they loved it. It was an age- and gender-specific program that was rough-and-tumble, high-energy, and highly structured—and it kept campers on the go the entire day.

Trail to Life Camp was located just outside the sleepy town of Greenwich in North Central Ohio. It was owned and operated by a group of Christian laymen who had a burden for reaching children and teens with the gospel of Jesus Christ. TTLC was unique in that it was an entirely faith-based ministry—meaning the camp ran solely on prayer and the faithful gifts of people. Because of this, each camper was charged a miniscule registration fee of two dollars for a full week of camp. It was to be a camp for anyone and everyone. As campers lined up at the registration tables in the mess hall, it didn't matter if they were street kids, gang members, farm kids, or wealthy suburban kids; they were now soldiers of Trail to Life Camp.

As soldiers of Trail to Life Camp, campers marched everywhere, saluted superior officers, and stood at attention for daily inspections. Campers were taught skills needed for wilderness camping: how to use a map and compass, tent pitching, first-aid, knot-tying, fire-building, axe and knife safety (as each camper was required to have a knife), along with canoeing and swimming. Add to this softball and soccer games, competing on the military obstacle course, and unbelievable water-balloon battles—some lasting until 2 a.m.— it's easy to understand why no one had trouble sleeping at night.

The love of God permeated every aspect of the program, and the gospel of Jesus Christ was clearly taught. The highlight of each day was the evening program. The squads (each cabin was a squad) would march to the lodge and stand at attention in company formation until given the order by Captain Don Enzor to go inside.

In the lodge the energy level of the meeting seemed to raise the roof. We would sing song after song at the top of our voices. Some were nonsense songs, while most were gospel songs and praise choruses. But the one song that was always sung with the most enthusiasm was the Trial to Life Camp song:

We are the soldiers from Trail to Life Camp,
We take our orders from the Lord.
We learn His Word each day,
We stop to kneel and pray,
We're in the army of the Lord.

About the time everyone's voices were hoarse from singing all out, a high-powered speaker would step to the microphone and give a gospel presentation, calling us to saving faith in Jesus Christ or to godly living and a full surrender of our lives to the Lord. My life was just one of the many that were transformed eternally during those evening meetings.

Every Friday was testing day. Following morning inspections and Bible class, the squads rotated through various testing stations. In the mess hall they faced a written exam that tested them on their canoeing, camping, and very basic first-aid knowledge. At headquarters, each private was handed a length of rope and told to tie a square knot, a taunt-line hitch, a two-half hitch, and a clove hitch. At the lakefront, each one was tested on his or her canoeing skills in both the bow and stern, demonstrating the ability to do canoeing strokes such as the J-stroke, the sweep stroke, and the draw stroke. The final station was the swimming area, where each private had to demonstrate to his sergeant the ability to swim at least ten yards.

These skills were taught every day, and the kids studied and worked hard to learn them. The reward for their efforts was huge. The top fifteen campers would win a weeklong, all-expense-paid canoeing trip in the Canadian wilderness of Algonquin Provincial Park in Ontario, Canada.

It had been a fantastic week at TTLC. This was my third year as a sergeant (counselor), and my squad had really come together as a team. Several of them had made commitments to the Lord. Even though we lost almost all our softball games, we did take first place in the canoe races and the fire-building contest, and we finished second in the squad obstacle course race and the tent-pitching competition.

Every night after my guys were asleep, I would quietly make my way down to the PX (snack shop) and meet up with my cousin Chuck and a good friend, Bob Scodova, for a bedtime snack of candy bars, potato chips, and suicides—our conglomeration of cola, orange soda, 7-Up, and root beer. There were those who accused us of being responsible for pulling various pranks during these outings—but I will neither confirm nor deny the accuracy of those reports—though Bob *was* "executed" via water-balloon firing squad for one such supposed crime. He "died" loyal to the cause and never gave up the names of possible accomplices.

In addition to all the fun and goofing around that was part of our evening ritual, our conversations always gravitated to what the Lord was doing in our lives or the lives of the guys in our squads. One evening, Bob shared about a private in his squad, Tim Meadows. "I don't know what to do. If there is anyone in my squad that deserves to go to Canada this year, it's Tim. He received Christ on Sunday night and has a voracious appetite for Bible knowledge. There is no one in my squad who tries harder, is more fun to be around, or has developed his camping and canoeing skills more than Tim."

"The problem is, he doesn't have a clue how to swim. I'm trying to teach him what little I know, but I don't think he's getting it."

"Remember, he is only required to swim ten yards any way he can," Chuck chimed in.

"That's right," I added. "It doesn't matter if he dog-paddles, floats, or lies on his back and kicks. He just has to cover ten yards."

"Well, I've got two days to get it done with Tim. He deserves to go," Bob concluded.

On Friday, the last night of Senior Boys Week, a couple of hours after taps and long after my squad was asleep, I was gently shaken awake. Speaking in a whisper, someone said to me, "Sergeant Miller, you are being tapped out to receive the Man of the Star Award. Please get dressed and follow me." A few moments later I stumbled out of the cabin, still tucking in my shirttails and pulling up my zipper, to find Lieutenants Mike Mecurio, Chet Weigle, and Howie Reinhold, all in their army-type uniforms, standing there. "Sergeant Miller, fall in and follow us."

We walked to an area next to the obstacle course where Captain

Don Enzor was standing by a campfire. I was called to attention and Lieutenant Chet Weigle spoke: "Sergeant Miller, you have been chosen to receive the Man of the Star Award. Please listen carefully to what this entails." He looked down at the certificate in his hands and read, "The Man of the Star Award is presented to you for meritorious service for outstanding service in the army of Christ, which includes: active faith in Christ, love for others, deep sincerity, diligence in all labor, honesty no matter the cost, consistent cooperation, always helpful to others, kindness to fellowman, cheerful no matter the circumstances, respectful of authority, and outstanding leadership."

When he finished, he looked me square in the eyes and asked, "Sergeant Miller, do you understand these qualifications and the inherent responsibilities they carry?"

"Yes, sir," I replied.

"Then please kneel so we can lay our hands on you and commit your life to whole-hearted service to our Lord Jesus Christ."

As I knelt there next to the fire and these men prayed for me, I began to sense the enormity of what it meant to be selected to be a Man of the Star and that I was being set apart to be a godly leader.

When the men had finished praying, Captain Don Enzor, spoke, "Sergeant Miller, rise. You are not to speak of this to anyone before the awards program tomorrow morning. Do you understand?"

"Yes sir," was my short reply.

"Congratulations! You are now a Man of the Star." With those words, Don stuck out his hand to shake mine, and with a smile that went from ear to ear, said, "I'm so proud of you!"

Receiving the Man of the Star Award was the fulfillment of a goal I had for several years. I couldn't believe it was now a reality. Hearing Don say that meant so much to me! He had been my hero and the person I wanted to be like more than anyone.

Don was my sergeant my first year at TTLC when I was eleven years old. We were in the cabin getting unpacked when he walked in, bigger than life, and barked out, "B-Squad, FALL IN!"

We quickly scrambled, half tripping over each other, as we piled out of the cabin to fall in—even though most of us had no idea what "fall in" meant. We lined up facing him as he called us to attention.

That was the week I realized my need to trust in Jesus as my Savior, and I prayed to do so after one of the evening programs. When I walked into the cabin afterwards, Don met me with a huge smile and boomed, "Where have you been, Miller?"

"I stayed after the meeting and talked with someone about how I can ask Jesus to be my Savior," I stammered, "and then I prayed and did it."

Don reached out and shook my hand while putting his other hand on my shoulder, and through a huge smile, bellowed, "That is fantastic!"

He was a man's man—strong, athletic, and friendly. Don's relationship with Jesus was so strong that after playing college football for a year, he walked away from it in order to devote himself entirely to his studies, including his independent studies of Bible and doctrine.

Don grew up in a godly home. This, coupled with a terrible tragedy that occurred when he was fifteen years old, gave Don the burning desire that shaped and drove his life.

On New Year's Day, 1962, Don was hunting predatory birds that were threatening his family's chickens. He saw a hawk land on a tree branch, took careful aim, fired his gun, but missed the bird. What he didn't know until later that day when the sheriff came to their house, was that his bullet came down a half mile away, striking an eight-year-old neighbor boy in the head, killing him.

Though it was ruled an accidental death, Don carried the burden of that memory the rest of his life—fanning into a large flame the realization that life is short and that he needed to tell as many people as he could about Jesus. Whenever he met someone, he would look for opportunities to tell him about Christ. Before long, his pastor saw a gift in Don and allowed him to preach on occasion. By the time he was in college, he was traveling around Ohio holding evangelistic services in churches.

In 1970, Don was hired as the first paid director of Trail to Life Camp. He and his wife, Twila, moved into a house he had built on the camp lake. During the off-season, he worked as an itinerant evangelist throughout Ohio.

Don had an ear-to-ear smile that lit up a room. His booming voice could be heard everywhere, yet it could become soft and compassionate when necessary. Though he often stuttered when speaking, no hint of an impediment existed when he sang. And, oh how he could sing!

Earlier that week at Senior Boys Week at TTLC, a sixteen-year-old camper who was a gang leader in his hometown was brought to Don because he had threatened his sergeant with his hunting knife. Don was sitting on a folding chair in headquarters and happened to be holding a canoe paddle when the teen was brought to him.

"So what seems to be the problem here, Private?" Don asked.

"I don't have a problem!" the camper snapped back. All talking in the headquarters instantly ceased, as everyone seemed to hold their breath—no one had ever talked to Captain Don in that tone of voice.

"Son, you need to check your attitude and sit down and tell me what's going on."

The camper yelled, "I don't have to do what you tell me!" as he pulled his knife out of its sheath and pointed it at Don.

In an instant, the camper found himself lying on the floor, and his knife was flying across the room. Don had smacked the canoe paddle across the boy's shoulder, knocking him off his feet.

Instead of calling the police or sending the teen home, Don helped him up, sat him in a chair, and talked with him. Before the conversation was over, Don had led the teen to faith in Jesus Christ. As the teen later shared in a testimony time, Don was the first person he couldn't intimidate and who beat him at his own game, yet showed real love and care for him. I had never heard of anyone compassionately witnessing with a canoe paddle before, but that was the kind of man Don Enzor was.

Saturday morning was a flurry of activity. Following breakfast, we were given an extra half-hour to prepare for final inspection. All sleeping bags and personal gear were packed up, carried down to the mess hall, and piled on our squad's table. Our cabin was swept clean, and the area around it was scoured for any candy wrappers or water balloon fragments that might still be lying around before we stood at attention for Captain Don's final inspection of the week.

After inspection, every squad marched down and stood in a single column formation in front of the mess hall for our closing ceremony. Captain Enzor then spoke. "Men, we've had a great week of camp, made some new friends and a lot of great memories. But what is most important is how you allowed the Lord to work in your life. Many of you are going home transformed because you are now children of God through your new faith in Jesus as your Savior. Others of you committed to living lives that are sold out to Jesus.

"In a few moments, we are going to be recognizing the Man of the Star recipient, as well as those of you who have earned the Canadian canoe trip. But those of you who now have salvation through Christ have something far greater than anything else we have to offer."

With those words, he paused and Lieutenant Chet Weigle called out, "Sergeant Duane Miller, front and center."

I snapped to attention and marched forward until I stood directly in front of the officers. I saluted them and said, "Sergeant Miller reporting as ordered, sir."

Captain Enzor spoke, "Sergeant Miller is the recipient of this year's Man of the Star Award. I want to read to you what is inscribed on the framed certificate we will be giving him in recognition of this achievement." He then proceeded to read it aloud.

He then said, "Sergeant Miller, it is with great honor we give you this certificate as a reminder to you to continue to develop these qualities throughout your life."

With those words, he reached out and shook my hand and ha.. me the plaque. "Fall back in with your squad."

I saluted him, did an about-face, and marched back to my former position as my squad broke out in applause and cheers. Then everyone else joined in to congratulate me.

The closing ceremony continued with the naming of the fifteen campers who had qualified for the wilderness canoe trip, as well as the three alternates who would go if any of the fifteen had to cancel. Tim Meadows did make the trip, as did my younger brother, Vernon. My cousin Chuck, Bob Scodova, and I were also going as sergeants, along with a fourth sergeant, Gary Kochheiser. Four lieutenants and Captain Enzor would provide the adult leadership.

When I drove out of the camp that day with my car radio cranked up and my passengers, Chuck and Vernon, singing along, I thought everything was going right in my life. I was seventeen years old and on top of the world. My framed Man of the Star certificate, which sat on the car seat next to me, reflected my smile every time I glanced down at it. As a senior at Firelands High School outside Oberlin, Ohio, I was overflowing with youthful naivety. Everything was going to happen just as I planned—play college football, marry my steady girlfriend Molly Brotherton, and return to teach and coach at Firelands.

What wasn't on my radar was how, in a few short days, the Canadian canoe trip we so eagerly anticipated would turn everything upside down and shake me to the very core.

CHAPTER TWO

EXERCISING "STUG"

"God is going to do something amazing on this trip!" Don Enzor sang out as we drove down the driveway of Trail to Life Camp. "Yeah!" we all shouted back as we pulled out of the camp driveway and onto the road in a station wagon packed full of anticipation and camping gear. We were barely out of the camp driveway when Tim Meadows, who was lying on a bed he had made on top of all our gear in the back of the station wagon, whined, "Are we there yet?" We laughed and pounded him with playful punches.

It was Saturday, July 18, 1970, and we were part of a group of twenty-three men and teenage boys (one teenager cancelled on the day of the trip) from Trail to Life Camp, packed into four station wagons, embarking on a weeklong canoeing adventure in the Canadian wilderness of Algonquin Provincial Park in Ontario, Canada. For us, it was the trip of a lifetime!

The five of us that piled into that station wagon were quite the conglomeration. Kim Graham, who had earned top camper of Senior Boys Week, was a well-known high school quarterback for a local school. He was tall and reserved. He always gave me the feeling he was observing everything going on around him and willing to step in and take charge if the situation needed it—kind of like a quarterback coming up to the line of scrimmage. Al DesChamps was a friend of mine from youth group at Church of the Open Door in Elyria, Ohio. He was average height, slender, with a quick wit and a big smile and was always ready for a good laugh. Tim Meadows was short in stature and built like a rock, yet was a quiet, shy kid with a great sense of humor and a kind heart. Don and I filled out our squad for the trip.

For me, this trip was going to be the trip of all trips. Although this was my third excursion to Algonquin, it was going to be my first time doing the "Big Loop"—a sixty-mile route of lakes, rivers, and portages (the paths we use when we must carry our canoes and supplies between lakes and around rapids). Adding to the excitement of the trip was the pride I felt for having been chosen to be in Don's squad. When the squads were announced just before we started loading the cars, a couple of the veterans of other trips gave me a friendly elbow and whispered, "Look who's the teacher's pet!"

We drove all day and traveled nearly 500 miles north and east to Huntsville, Ontario. After grabbing a bite to eat, we drove to a small roadside rest area outside of Huntsville, where some of us unrolled our sleeping bags and fell asleep on the grass while others sacked out in the cars for the night. We were up and going before sunrise the next morning. After grabbing a quick breakfast at a small diner, we drove the remaining two hours—much of it on gravel roads—to Opeongo Lake in the heart of Algonquin Provincial Park.

Opeongo Lake, the largest lake in Algonquin Provincial Park, is deceptively dangerous. It's shaped in the rough form of a "Y" with many islands, coves, and bays, and it has about 108 miles of shoreline. On a calm day, it can lure you into complacency with its beauty, but it also can be very temperamental, quickly turning into a caldron of choppy waves three to three-and-a-half-feet high. It has claimed more lives through the years than any other lake in Algonquin Park.

Upon arrival at the outfitters at the southern end of Opeongo, we were shocked by the poor quality of the canoes available to rent. Don had called the outfitter weeks earlier to reserve eight, seventeen-foot fiberglass canoes for our trip. However, when Don and the leaders were shown the hodge-podge of canoes that had been set aside for us, they were upset. The canoes were beat up and looked abused, plus some were aluminum, which weighed about fifteen pounds more than the fiberglass. But worst of all, one of the canoes was only sixteen feet long—not big enough to carry three teenagers and their gear in rough weather.

"Wait a minute," Don protested. "These aren't the canoes we reserved. We're supposed to have seventeen-footers. Some of these are in terrible condition and you promised us fiberglass. What good is it to make reservations if this is what we get?"

The outfitter shrugged his shoulders, "Well, these are all that are available today. I guess you can try to find another outfitter. But good luck in finding one that could get eight, seventeen-foot fiberglass canoes here today."

We were stuck. If we didn't rent these canoes, it could take hours, if not the entire day, to find another outfitter who could rent and deliver the canoes to the dock on the south end of Opeongo Lake.

Don and the lieutenants had a short discussion among themselves before Don turned to the outfitter, "I guess we don't have any other choice. We'll take them."

Though it seemed to be the expedient thing to do, we didn't know how heavily this decision would play into future events.

Tim, Al, and I grabbed our canoe and carried it to the dock where we put it in the water and tied it to the dock. I climbed into the canoe as Tim started to hand me a backpack. "Wait a minute," I called out. "Al, grab the gunnel and hold on to steady the canoe while we load. I don't want to swamp the canoe while still tied to the dock!"

I put both the duffle bag with our food in it and the backpack with the cooking utensils and tent in the section of the canoe just behind the middle thwart. Then I stowed the backpack with our sleeping bags and personal bags in the area just behind the bow seat parallel with the canoe.

"You two will be switching off paddling in the bow and straddling this pack like a horse while you paddle," I explained. "With this wind today, all three of us are going to need to be paddling." I dropped one lifejacket in the stern of the canoe so I could kneel on it while paddling. The main reason I brought the lifejacket was so I would have some padding for my shoulders when I carried our canoe on the portages. In those days, Canadian law did not require lifejackets in canoes since canoes inherently have enough buoyancy to keep paddlers above water if they should capsize.

The tension at the dock caused by the problem of getting inadequate canoes set the stage for what was going to be an extremely hard day. As we settled into our canoe and prepared to pull away from the dock, a driving, sideways, in-your-face deluge of rain began. While we donned our rain ponchos, Al called out in a Jamaican accent, "No problem, mon! We are soldiers from Trail to Life Camp!"

As we made the turn into the main channel of Opeongo Lake, we were met with a strong headwind. We tried to stay out of the wind by skirting along the edge of the lake and taking advantage of the lee side of Bates Island, but the wind really slowed our progress. It was noon before we were able to make it to Windy Point peninsula, where we stopped to stretch our legs and eat lunch. After filling our bellies with peanut butter and jelly sandwiches, trail mix, and Tang, we loaded up to head out into one of the most challenging parts of Opeongo Lake. We soon learned that the name Windy Point was extremely accurate.

Windy Point overlooks the area where Opeongo Lake separates into the two arms of a "Y," and for whatever the reason, the wind seems to always be blowing across that stretch of water. There would be no shores to skirt, no islands to break the force of the wind, only sheer determination, canoeing abilities, and "stug" would get us across. "Stug" is *guts* spelled backwards, and it is a term someone in another canoe came up with that day to describe our "I-can't-possibly-take-one-more-stroke-without-my-arms-falling-off-but-I-can't-quit-so-I'm-going-to-keep-paddling" determination.

If we had not persevered that day as we paddled into the strong head wind, we would have been at the mercy of the power of the wind and waves. But we did persevere, and we did overcome the challenges they threw at us. We did so by following two fundamental canoeing principles: we kept paddling, and we kept our eyes on our destination.

Paddling into the headwind, I knew how vital that first principle was—keep paddling. Keeping our momentum was key to controlling our canoe. If we stopped paddling, the wind and waves would instantly gain control, taking us where we didn't want to go and possibly capsizing us.

So I began calling out the cadence, "Stug ... stug ... stug" at the beginning of each stroke so we would stay in rhythm and maximize the synergy of each stroke. Occasionally, one of us would switch up the cadence with a new one like, "I ... like ... pain" or "I ... want ... my ... mommy."

With Al and Tim paddling on the same side, and me paddling on the opposite side, we made steady headway. Every five or six minutes, one of us would cry out, "I need a break!" I would then call out, "Ready ... switch ... (switch sides) ... stug ... stug," and in unison, we would all change paddling sides to give our arms a rest while maintaining our rhythm and momentum.

Stug requires having a never-give-up attitude.

The second fundamental principle of canoeing we followed was keeping our eyes on our destination. Every time we loaded into our canoes to head out after a break, someone would call out, "Where are we heading now, Captain?" Don would reply, "See that island," or "Head for that peninsula," or whatever landmark would serve as a beacon for us. Sometimes, though, he would simply say, "Follow me." Once we knew where we were headed, we stayed focused on it and kept the bows of our canoes pointed at it.

As we paddled into the waves, the spray from the waves breaking against the canoe hit our faces, and repeatedly we felt the bow of the canoe drop as it went down the backside of a wave. The temptation was to look down and focus on everything that was happening around us, which would mean taking our eyes off our destination and putting us at risk of being blown off course. Looking down and watching the waves would also confuse us about our progress and discourage us. We couldn't tell if we were making any headway. But by looking up and keeping our destination in sight, we stayed on course and could see the slow but steady headway we were making.

After battling our way across the Windy Point area, we entered a narrower channel with several islands that provided a reprieve from the wind and waves. We pulled into one of the islands to take a break and rest our weary arms and shoulders. As we climbed out of our canoes, our ankles felt like steel wedges had been driven into them, our toes were asleep, and we weren't sure if our knees would ever straighten out again. With all our focus on the wind and waves, we hadn't thought to occasionally shift our weight to keep the circulation in our legs flowing. Fortunately, after simply standing and moving around a bit, we began to regain use of all our extremities.

All too soon Don called out the order, "Load 'em up, move 'em out!" We all responded with enthusiastic moans and groans. The wind and waves again greeted us as we paddled past the shelter of the island.

Long distance runners talk about "hitting the wall." It's that point during a run when all energy is spent, the legs feel like rubber, and the mind screams, "Stop!" But if runners persevere through the "wall" and run in spite of exhaustion, suddenly strength and energy are renewed, and they are able to finish strong. As we entered the North Arm of Opeongo Lake, the wind was just as powerful and the waves just as big as before. But we had hit the wall and persevered. Suddenly, a surge of renewed energy came over us, and we were able to finish strong.

Finally, the northern shore of the lake was right before us. We had arrived at our destination: the beginning of the portage to Proulx

Lake. We wanted to cheer, but all we could muster were sighs of "We made it." We turned the canoe to the right and quietly entered into a protective cove where the trail started. Tim and Al laid their paddles down and slumped forward in exhaustion, so I called out to them, "Guys, don't quit on me yet. I need two more minutes of paddling out of you if we are going to make it to shore." As we slowly glided to shore, a feeling of having conquered an overwhelming foe enveloped us. We had persevered, we had overcome, and it felt good.

It didn't matter that it had taken us eight hours to paddle what should have only taken three-and-a-half to four hours for a group our size. We had made it. Stug had paid off, and the twelve miles of Opeongo Lake were behind us.

We climbed out of our canoes and pulled them partway onto shore and collapsed on the ground. Don and several of the other adults walked through the woods next to the trail and decided we would make that area our campsite for the night.

Soaked to the skin, cold, and exhausted, no one complained when they came back and Don announced, "We are camping here tonight." Our tents were quickly pitched, firewood cut, campfires roaring, and spirits lifted as we filled our stomachs with a hearty, hot meal. We were in the wilderness and loving it.

CHAPTER THREE

THINGS DON'T GO WRONG, THEY ONLY GO DIFFERENT

We woke early the next morning to the realization that we were in trouble.

The night before, Tim, Al, and I had carefully pitched our tent. We had chosen a level spot, carried in about six inches of pine needles for padding and insulation under our tent, and dug a small trench around it to drain the rainwater away.

Exhausted, we climbed into the tent that night feeling dry, warm, and snug. We had done everything right to insure a good night's sleep, but these were the days before lightweight nylon tents with rain flies. Our tents were three-man canvas pup tents without rain flies. Because we didn't have that second layer of the tent roof deflecting the rain, if we would simply touch the inside of the tent while it was raining, the water would wick through the canvas and drip on the occupants.

Consequently, we learned that combining an all-night rain and a canvas tent with three tossing and turning teenage boys equals total wetness. Our tent went from a refuge of warmth and dryness to being as effective as a sieve. Fortunately for me, I slept in the middle. Being elbowed and jabbed every time one of the other guys rolled over was a small price to pay to have a dry sleeping bag. Only the foot of my sleeping bag was wet, but Tim's and Al's sleeping bags were drenched as a result of rubbing against the sides of the tent.

I was awakened at first light to the sound of Al and Tim complaining, "Oh man, my sleeping bag is soaked."

"Too bad," I replied, "but I stopped wetting the bed years ago!" Which earned me a barrage of elbows and punches in the ribs.

We could not get dressed and out of the tent fast enough so we could get the fire going. I dug into the coals under a piece of wood in our fire pit and found a couple of hot coals. I took a few tissue-paper-thin pieces of birch bark and held them against the coals and blew on them through chattering teeth until a flame sprang up. Soon we had a roaring fire, and the chill started to leave our bones. About that time, Don and Kim crawled out of their tent and joined us. "Nice of you two sleepy heads to join us," Al kidded, "now that the fire is going."

As the other squads began emerging from their tents, we discovered that having dripping tents was a unifying experience. Everyone was cold and wet. It was evident that we were in no condition to finish the 60-mile loop of lakes and rivers we had hoped to travel. Don called the lieutenants and sergeants together to discuss our situation.

"It seems that we all got wet last night and are in no condition to press on with our original plans. What do the rest of you think?" Don asked.

Bob Scodova spoke up in defense of pushing on. "What's a little rain? Let's at least move on to Big Crow Lake. If it is still raining when we get there, then we can decide."

Though most of us wanted to agree with Bob, each of us knew in our gut that staying put was the right thing to do. There seemed to be a consensus, so Don made the call, "We'll stay here today and not do the big loop." Crow River, Lake Lavielle, Dickson Lake, and the East Arm of Opeongo Lake would have to wait for another trip and another year.

Unwilling to completely surrender to the rain, our new plan was to stay put for one more night, portage to Proulx Lake, and then paddle to Big Crow Lake. Several of us had been to Big Crow Lake and knew it was a good alternative destination. There was a lot to see and do there: beautiful, soft, sandy beaches, an active fire tower and ranger cabin, a mountain spring with ice cold, sweet water, and the ruins of a logging camp from the 1800s—not to mention a nearby virgin white pine forest to explore—provided more than enough to see and do at that lake. We would spend two nights there and then head back.

With the decision made to stay put, we set about to make the best of our soggy situation. Each squad developed its own campsite. We had chosen a level area about fifty feet from the portage trail to pitch our tents and build a fire. Over a warm breakfast of oatmeal and hot chocolate, Kim, Al, Tim, and I discussed how we could further develop our site to provide additional warmth and protection from the rain and cool temperature.

I think it was Kim who came up with the idea of turning our canoes upside down and using them for shelter: one for protecting our gear and firewood and the other to provide shelter for us. Once we agreed on the concept, the ideas started to flow as our project took shape mostly through trial and error with everyone joining in the conversation.

"If we use forked sticks like these, we can prop up one side of the canoe to give us more head room."

"There's still a lot of air blowing under the canoe, let's pile pine needles against the back of the canoe and put some firewood on them to block the wind."

"I think that if we build a wall of rocks around this side of the fire pit, it will protect the fire from the wind and reflect heat into our canoe shelter."

We finished off our shelter with a couple of inches of pine needles under the canoe to keep us from sitting on the wet ground.

The other squads were also in the process of building lean-tos and shelters. As time went on, a hodge-podge of shelters began to emerge. One squad tied a rope between two trees and leaned their canoes upside-down on it. Another squad was very ambitious and built a framework and covered the roof with strips of birch bark and the sides with pine boughs. The last squad couldn't seem to get any idea to work, so after several failed attempts they gave up and invaded the other shelters.

We knew our shelter would not win any awards for looks—what beauty is there in an upside-down gray canoe and sticks? But it was home: functional and warm. It was low enough for the smoke to go over the top, but it allowed for the heat from the fire to reflect into our shelter and circulate. We had to crawl on our hands and knees to get into it, but we had a place to sit that was out of the rain and dry. That was all we wanted.

We had just finished building it and crawled into it when the skies again opened up and poured on us. We moaned, "Is this ever going to stop?" "I've never been so sick of rain." But no sooner had we started our pity party than Tim came walking into camp looking like a miniature Paul Bunyan in a rain poncho, dragging an entire dead pine tree that he had chopped down. It was about twenty-five-feet long. He was grinning ear from ear and was having too much fun to let the rain bother him.

Seeing him ended our grumbling session. We climbed out of our shelter and joined him in cutting the tree up. Soon we were laughing and joking as our mountain of cut firewood grew.

Don had wandered away from our campsite while we were putting our shelter together. He had been checking on how everyone else was doing. He had a good laugh when he came back and saw our shelter—especially when he tried to climb under the canoe. His football body didn't fit. He had to curl up in a ball and even then his legs stuck out.

"Who came up with this idea?" he asked.

"Hey, Kim," I replied with a wink, "isn't it interesting that the fan in the stands is always the loudest critic of those of us who are actually playing the game?"

Tim joined in the banter, "Yeah, Don, how are things up in the peanut gallery?"

"You guys are too much," Don retorted. "I'm going to a shelter that fits!"

Once he left, Kim spoke up, "You know, we probably should modify our shelter so Don can sit in it. After all, he is our leader!"

He had a point, so after a short discussion and a few failed attempts, Tim came up with the game-winning idea. "Why don't we try laying the second canoe upside down, perpendicular to the first canoe, and lay its bow on top of the other canoe?"

The idea worked. It provided a seat with a lot more head and legroom without losing any of the space we needed to stack some of our firewood out of the rain.

All of these experiences—as wet and cold as they happened to be—were drawing us all closer. Building the shelter and chopping the firewood not only kept us busy but also gave us a chance to talk and get to know each other better. As we worked, we started sharing how Christ had changed our lives.

This got Tim talking. He had been very quiet throughout the trip, but when he started talking about Jesus, his face lit up and the words flowed from him. He shared how less than a year before, his dad came home from work one night and announced to the family:

"The people over at Union Baptist Church are having special meetings this week and we're going tonight, so get ready."

"This was a shock to everyone. My family had never had anything to do with church. But this was just like Dad—he saw everything in black and white. When he thought something needed to be done, it was done, period. So a short time later my whole family filed into the church and filled an entire church pew.

"That evening we heard the gospel message for the first time.

Dad went forward during the altar call and received Christ as his Savior. His conversion was dramatic. As he told the pastor when he was asked why he had come forward, 'If I'm a sinner destined for hell, and Jesus is offering to save me, I'd be a fool not to accept His offer.'

"That evening, when we got home, Dad announced: 'I'm a Christian now and even though I don't know what all happened to me, I know I'm different inside. So things are going to change around here. I'm not going to be drinking or cussing anymore and we are all going to go to church from now on.'"

From that moment on, Tim's dad, Ray Meadows, lived a zealous life for Jesus.

Tim went on, "Several months later, Don Enzor spoke at a series of evangelistic services at our church. He kept telling us about Trail to Life Camp. The more he talked about it, the more I wanted to go. It took some time to convince my parents, because my dad didn't want to accept charity. But when he found out that they would accept produce from our garden as payment, I was allowed to go."

That is why a few months later, the entire Meadows family, Dad, Mom (Dixie), Tim, and his four brothers and two sisters, piled out of their station wagon at Trail to Life Camp to drop Tim off for Senior Boys Week. It was to be a week where Tim encountered the Lord Jesus Christ in a powerful and personal way.

Whereas his dad had come to Jesus in a simple, black-and-white understanding of the gospel, Tim met Him in full living color. The impact of the love, grace, and mercy of God the Father for him overwhelmed his heart. He had watched how the Lord had changed his dad, and now it was his time to be transformed by faith in Jesus.

The change in Tim was immediate. The Lord gave him a heart of compassion and sensitivity coupled with a broken heart for those who didn't know Jesus. He couldn't wait to get home and tell people about Jesus.

There were two weeks between camp and the canoe trip. During that time, Tim told everyone he could about Jesus, and he led several people, including a couple of family members, to faith in Jesus as their Savior. His faith in Christ wasn't a religion for him but a life-transforming relationship with the Almighty God, who loved him with an infinite love. He felt the Lord was calling him to be a missionary, and he was excited about the prospects of serving the Lord.

We had worked hard all morning upgrading our campsite, making and modifying our shelter, and cutting a large pile of firewood, so when noon came we were hungry. While Kim and Al filled our water jugs and soaped the outside of our pots, Tim and I let our food packs down from where they were suspended in the trees. A reality of wilderness camping is the presence of bears. So we had suspended our food pack between two trees and about eight feet from the ground to protect it from bears.

It wasn't long before we were all sitting around the fire enjoying some hot soup and peanut butter and jelly sandwiches.

Just about the time I was losing the argument over whether or not it was my turn to do the dishes, my cousin, Chuck, walked into our camp.

"Hey Duane, Scodova and I are going to go over to Proulx Lake and explore it," Chuck said. "Do you want to join us?"

"Naw, I can't. I'm up for doing the dishes. Find someone else to go." I replied, which was only partly true. The real reason I didn't want to go was I wanted to take a nap, but I would never admit that to my cousin. He would never let me hear the end of it!

"Okay," Chuck said as he turned to walk away. "Your loss."

After the adventurers left, we began to clean up. Al and I had finished washing the dishes, and we were starting to get things organized so we could hang the food back up in the trees when we heard voices of people coming from the portage. Crossing paths with another group in the wilderness rarely happens, so we went over to greet them.

What we saw shocked us. Three men and six ten-year-old boys stumbled toward us. The men each carried a canoe on their shoulders and a small backpack, while each of the boys struggled under the weight of his backpack.

The boys wore shorts and sweatshirts that were soaked through. They were shaking almost uncontrollably and their teeth were chattering. Their skin was very pale, and all the boys were coughing.

They had been in the interior for several days, the last two being days of cold weather, relentless wind, and endless rain. To make matters worse, none of them knew how to start a fire in the rain and none had decent rain gear. They only had cold, uncooked food to eat and no way to get warm or dry.

As soon as we saw them, we invited them to join us at our campfires. One of the boys came to our campsite and climbed into our shelter. Since our food was still in the campsite, we had hot food ready in no time. Whatever we cooked, he devoured instantly, while drinking cup after cup of hot chocolate.

Meanwhile, the adults in our group gathered with the three men at one of the other sites for lunch. While they sat together under the lean-to at that site, the conversation became intense. I could hear their voices in our campsite. I looked over toward where the noise was coming from just in time to see Mike Mercurio, who was a high school principal, stand up and shout, "What were you thinking, bringing these kids out into the wilderness without rain gear?"

Another lieutenant joined in and shouted, "And you didn't even take the time before the trip to learn how to start a fire in the rain?"

"Your own stupidity put the boys' lives, not to mention your own lives, at risk," Mike continued with the intensity he would have had if he had caught a student trying to start a fire in the school restroom.

By this time, the three men were on their feet, almost toe to toe with our leaders.

"Shut up!" they shouted. "You have no business talking to us like that! Do you think that we are blind and can't see how serious our situation is?"

With that, Don spoke up, "You're right. We had no right to yell at you that way and we apologize. What is done is done. But the reality is this; you can't survive out here without knowing how to start a fire. How can we help you? Would you like us to show you how to start a fire in the rain? We'd be happy to teach you."

Don's offer quelled the argument. Soon each man in the group was building a fire in the rain under the guidance of our leaders.

The boy at our campsite began to warm up and dry off. As we talked with him, I remembered something Don had drilled into us at camp—to learn to look for opportunities to share the gospel. If we learn to look for them, we will discover them everywhere. I looked at the boy sitting there under our canoe-shelter, who just happened to walk into our camp wet and hungry, and I thought, *Maybe this is one of those opportunities Don had talked about!*

I had never initiated a discussion with anyone before with the purpose of sharing the gospel, but I felt it was what the Lord wanted me to do. I happened to have in my shirt pocket a TTLC gospel tract Don had written. It was wet and limp but legible, so as we sat together under the canoe shelter, I took a deep breath and stammered: "Do you know Jesus as your Savior?"

"I don't know what you mean," he replied.

"Well, I have a tract here that explains it. Can I read it to you?" I said as I pulled the wet paper out of my shirt pocket and carefully opened it so as to not tear it.

The boy shrugged and said, "Sure, why not."

So I nervously read the tract to him, word for word. When I came to the end, there was a suggested prayer that a person could pray that expressed the truths talked about in the tract. It was a prayer of repentance and belief in the sacrificial death and resurrection of Jesus Christ, expressing faith in Jesus as Savior.

I stopped and looked at the boy and asked, "Do you understand everything I have just told you?

The boy shook his head yes.

"Would you like to receive Jesus as your personal Savior?"

He looked at me and said, "Yes, I would."

We bowed our heads, I led him in a prayer of faith, and he became a child of God.

We finished praying and he looked up, smiling. "That is so neat!" he exclaimed.

A couple of hours after arriving, the group was ready to move on. With full bellies, warm bodies, and dry clothes, they listened as we prayed with them and sent them on their way. We gave them garbage bags with arm and neck holes cut into them as makeshift rain ponchos. We also supplied the leaders with a bag of stick matches that had been dipped in hot wax to make them waterproof. Later that evening, I found out another boy had also prayed to trust Christ as his Savior.

About an hour after the group of men and boys had left, the three adventurers, Chuck, Bob Scodova, and one other camper, Don Love, returned and came straight to our campsite, higher than a kite.

They all started talking at the same time, saying random things that didn't seem to make sense at first: "We almost died out there ... that tree almost fell right on us ... if we hadn't stopped when we did ... I've never been so sacred in my life!"

"Whoa! Slow down. Take a breath and tell us what happened— but don't all of you talk at once," someone suggested.

That stopped the barrage of talking, but they looked like they were going to explode if they had to keep quiet.

Chuck immediately spoke up, "We canoed to the other end of Proulx Lake and found an access road entrance. We decided to see where it led, so we followed the one lane dirt road for a while ..."

Bob interrupted, "—when suddenly there was a loud crack that sounded like a gun being fired!"

Chuck continued, "All three of us instantly stopped in our tracks."

"Then this huge dead tree fell across the road right in front of us!" All three of them shouted together, as if on cue: "If we had taken one more step, it would have landed right on us!"

"God stepped in and stopped us!" Chuck exclaimed. "He protected us. It's as if he was telling us not to worry. He is taking care of us, and today is not our day to die!"

What were the chances of these things just happening? The Lord's protection of the adventurers, as well as making both physical and spiritual salvation available to a group of strangers, was neither coincidence nor luck. We weren't even supposed to be there. If we had been able to stay on our schedule, we would have been camped on another lake miles away and neither incident would have happened. Yet we were at exactly the right spot in the wilderness of Canada, at the right time, to see of God's protection demonstrated and to have the awesome experience of sharing the love of Jesus Christ in tangible ways to a bunch of guys in need. God had arranged a divine appointment, and we had the privilege of being a part of it.

I was starting to see how the sovereignty of God affected our day-to-day lives. I was beginning to learn this truth: Because God is God and He is reigning from His throne in heaven, things don't go wrong; they only go different. "For my thoughts are not your thoughts, neither are your ways my ways, declares the LORD. For as the heavens are higher than the earth, so are my ways higher than your ways and my thoughts than your thoughts" (Isaiah 55:8–9).

Some time later, as we were beginning to cook dinner, Mike Mecurio, the co-leader of the trip, walked into our campsite.

"Do any of you know where Don is? I need to talk with him."

"I think he's sleeping in his tent," Kim replied, pointing to the tent.

Mike was concerned because a couple of the guys were getting sick, and the storm wasn't letting up. He turned and walked over to the tent and shook it, "Hey Don, you in there?"

"Yeah, I'm here, " came the reply. "What's up?"

"I need to talk with you. Can I come in?"

When Mike climbed into the tent, he was surprised by what he saw—he knew something was wrong. Don's eyes were red, as if he had been crying. "Are you okay?" Mike asked.

"I feel like Jacob when he wrestled with the Angel of the Lord all night, Mike. I have never been through what I just experienced. I've been overwhelmed with a huge sense of foreboding. I know something is going to happen, but I don't know what, and I've been crying out to God about it."

They talked, wept, and prayed about the situation and about what Don was sensing the Lord impressing on him. They also talked about Mike's concerns about the health and spirits of the guys. Mike wanted to organize something for the guys to do—to go exploring, or have some type of contest—to get their minds off the weather.

After a while, they prayed together for wisdom in what to do. When they finished, Don spoke, "I think we need to head back tomorrow morning. With kids getting sick and this weather not letting up, I feel it's the right thing to do." Mike nodded in agreement.

As Mike started to turn to crawl out of the tent, Don put his hand on Mike's shoulder and said, "Thanks. It really helped to be able to talk all this through with you. Don't tell anyone about our decision until I come out. I think it's best that we tell everyone together, but I need to spend some time talking with the Lord about this sense of foreboding. I'll be out in a bit."

With that, Mike turned and crawled out of the tent.

Later that evening, Don and Mike called everyone together. Don spoke up. "This storm is not letting up and we have people getting sick. So unless there is a dramatic turnaround in the weather, we will be heading back in the morning. I don't like this any more than the rest of you, but we've got to do what we've got to do."

The news was met by half-hearted boos and moans, but deep down, most of us realized we didn't have any other option. Only Bob raised a strong objection. "No! We need to press on. We are forgetting who we are—soldiers of Trail to Life Camp. We don't let a little rain stop us. We are not quitters."

But in spite of his objections, the decision to head home in the morning stuck.

When bedtime arrived, we found the inside of our tent still wet, forcing us to take two-hour shifts sleeping in the one semi-dry sleeping bag we had left. The other two sat outside with rain ponchos on and huddled under the shelter next to the campfire, occasionally dozing off, sleeping until our heads jerked or we tipped over and woke up. Since we were heading back in the morning, we didn't bother hanging the food pack back in the tree. Instead, we quietly cooked, ate, and dozed our way through what seemed to be an endless night. I don't think I have ever consumed so much hot chocolate or eaten as much canned beef stew, Spam, and instant pudding as I did that night.

By first light everyone was awake, cold, wet, and grumpy: We'd had more than our fill of this liquid sunshine. None of us complained when Don went through the sites and gave the order to break camp, because we knew that warm, dry clothes were waiting for us back at the cars. Only twelve miles of canoeing separated us from them.

So after a hearty breakfast, we packed up, loaded our canoes, and started our return trip down Opeongo Lake. We had no idea what was in store for us.

CHAPTER FOUR

THE DAY MY LIFE CHANGED

The fury of the storm surprised us as we emerged from the safety of the protective cove where we had camped. The wind was stronger and the waves bigger than we had anticipated. We paddled on the lee side of two large islands before stopping to decide if we should proceed. As we drifted close to the islands, I put my hand down in the water.

"I can't believe how warm the water feels compared to this cold, damp wind," I commented to Al and Tim.

They each stuck their hands in the water and responded, "You're right."

Before us lay the most threatening and dangerous stretch of water in Algonquin Park: the North Arm of Opeongo Lake. It is a large, open expanse of water that is almost four miles in diameter at its widest point and is surrounded by high hills. It is a notoriously challenging stretch of water.

As I looked out across the lake and the waves, a knot grew in my stomach. Canoeing in waves was nothing new for me. Three years earlier, my older brother, David, and I had pooled our resources and bought a canoe. Many late winter and spring Sunday afternoons would find us shooting the rapids on the Vermilion River that bordered our family farm—often when the river was swollen over its banks with snow melt. When summer came, the waves of Lake Erie off the beach of Linwood Park in Vermilion, Ohio, became our playground. Sometimes we had to swim out past the breakers and climb into the canoe in deep water because the waves were four feet high. It was thrilling to bust through a whitecap and feel the canoe drop out from under me as it plunged down the backside of the wave. Needless to say, we would often find ourselves unexpectedly swimming instead of canoeing after going into a big wave at the wrong angle.

Those experiences taught me an important principle about canoeing in waves: respect the waves and have fun, disrespect the waves and go swimming. Paddling directly into the waves is a blast, but the person in the bow gets soaked as the front of the canoe plunges into the front of the waves and water pours over the bow. Paddling diagonal to the waves is the safest and driest route to take. However, to paddle parallel with the waves is asking for trouble. The extreme rocking of the canoe and the power of a whitecap breaking against the sides can actually throw a person out or capsize the canoe.

Someone called out, "Where are we headed, captain?"

Don yelled back, "The shortest route is a straight line, so head for that tiny island," as he pointed to a small island at the far end of the North Arm of Opeongo.

As I looked out over the expanse of water, I knew in my gut that paddling across it was a bad idea. We would be paddling parallel to the waves. Why we didn't circumvent the North Arm, or at least take a zigzag route, I will never know.

On our first day we had encountered strong headwinds, but we overcame them with stug. However, on this day, determination and perseverance didn't change the level of danger we faced. There are those who claim that if you believe it, you can achieve it, but no amount of positive thinking could change the ominous waves and the punishing winds blowing from our right to our left.

Mike Mecurio paddled up to Don's canoe. "It really looks bad out there, Don."

"Maybe so," Don replied, "but I think our guys can handle it."

A couple of minutes later, Don called out, "Let's go!" and we headed out. I was terrified. On Lake Erie, we always had an empty canoe, wore life jackets, and stayed within a hundred yards of shore when the waves were big. On this day, our canoe was heavily loaded and handled like a log. Plus, there was just something about the waves and wind that turned my stomach. But since I was seventeen and a sergeant on this trip, I didn't want to look like a wimp. I was supposed to be a leader, and leaders lead—even when faced with danger. So I kept my mouth shut and joined in with everyone calling out in cadence "Stug! Stug! Stug!" to keep the pace of our paddle strokes in rhythm.

Being the partner canoe with Don's would have put me in the front of the two columns of canoes.

"Miller, I want you to hang back," Don shouted to me over the sound of the wind as we started out. "Help bring up the rear with any canoes that struggle."

Coming around the second island, the wind seemed to really pick up, creating choppy waves to reach a height of about three feet. Whitecaps continually hit us broadside. Each wave would pick us up, rocking us to the left, and when we reached the top of the wave, we would be rocked to the right—unless a whitecap hit us—then we would be suddenly thrown back to the left and a little water would splash into the canoe. Kneeling in the canoe helped us deal with the rocking the waves caused, and keeping our paddles in the water, stroking in rhythm, helped brace the canoe against the waves.

The light rain stung our faces as we plowed ahead into the waves. The wind, the waves, and the poor quality of the canoes, as well as the inexperience of many of the guys in canoeing in these conditions, created a recipe for disaster.

One canoe seemed to really struggle in the waves. It was the canoe with Chuck; my younger brother, Vernon; and Dan Barnhill in it. Dan had become sick the day before, was running a low fever, and felt very weak. In addition, they had the sixteen-foot canoe—the worst canoe in our group. It was not designed to carry three people plus gear. It rode low in the water and was unstable in the waves—making it difficult to handle. Chuck was in the stern and was struggling to handle the waves. His canoe had dropped to the back, so he and his crew were a little bit behind us and about ten yards to the right of my canoe. Suddenly, we heard their screams for help. They had taken a wave over the side and their canoe had swamped—filling their canoe with water, turning it on its side, and plunging all three of them into the frigid lake.

Chuck and Dan were able to roll out of the canoe as it continued to roll upside down, but Vernon's work boots caught on the underside of the canoe seat—pulling him underwater with the canoe holding him down. Just before he went under he let out a shout, "Hey!"

"Vernon's stuck!" Chuck yelled. "Turn the canoe over!"

They quickly rolled the canoe upright to allow my brother to free his feet from the canoe.

Tim and Al both blew the emergency whistles they had around their necks with all their might while I yelled for help to the closest canoe, which was Bob's. They passed the call for help up the line to Don. Bob and Don both turned their canoes around to help us rescue Chuck, Dan, and Vernon. The guys in the other four canoes continued paddling toward the small island that lay ahead with the intent of having tents, warm food, and dry clothes waiting for the guys after they were rescued.

My canoe was the first to reach Chuck's swamped canoe. Everyone was scared—but okay. As we pulled up alongside, I yelled, "Hey, the middle of the lake is no place to go swimming. You know the rules, no swimming until we get to the campsite."

Al joined in. "I sure hope the toilet paper isn't in your canoe, or it's leaves for all of us."

As Don's canoe arrived, he pulled alongside my canoe, which was next to the swamped canoe.

"Grab hold of the gunnels and thwarts of the canoe," Don and I called out to our guys. We reached over and grabbed the other canoe, pulling our canoes against each other. This steadied our canoes against the waves and kept them from tipping, enabling the guys to climb into the canoes. As Al and I hung onto Don's canoe, Tim reached over the edge of our canoe and helped Vernon climb in.

"Chuck and Dan, I've got room for both of you," Don yelled. "Swim around to the other side of my canoe and climb in."

While all this was going on, Bob was maneuvering his canoe around so his guys could pull backpacks and personal gear out of the water.

As soon as everyone was on board, we started paddling toward the small island where the rest of our group was headed. Don and I each had four people aboard, plus our wet gear. Bob's canoe had three people: himself, Wes Sperr, and Jerry Kochheiser, along with the extra gear they had pulled out of the water. All three canoes were riding dangerously low in the water, making it harder to rock with the waves. This made us more vulnerable to the impact of the white-caps, allowing more water to splash into the canoe, which in turn, put us lower in the water. With each stroke of my paddle, I no longer called out "Stug" but silently cried out, "Lord, help us!"

We had paddled only about a hundred yards when my canoe was hit by a whitecap that seemed to just roll over the edge of the canoe, filling us with water.

"Help us! We're going down! Help!" came the cries from our canoe.

The canoe rolled to the left as we scrambled to climb out and grab hold of the canoe gunnel so we could use the built-in floatation of the canoe as our life preserver. With guys hanging on both sides of the canoe to counterbalance it, we could let the buoyancy of the canoe hold us up. Al's boot got caught under his seat, but it was untied, so he was able to slip out of it. As soon as I was in the water, I was surprised with how cold the water was. This wasn't the warm water I had felt earlier. Now that we were in it, it was bone-chilling cold.

Don and Bob immediately turned around to help us.

As soon as we went into the water, I knew I needed to get rid of some of my clothes. I shed my rain poncho without much trouble, but my hiking boots were weighing me down, and they made treading water almost impossible. While hanging onto my swamped canoe, I untied one of my shoes and kicked it off. However, the shoelaces on the other shoe became knotted, so I couldn't get that shoe off. Every attempt to untie the shoe failed, so I hung onto my canoe along with Tim, Al, and Vernon, and we waited for Don and Bob to come get us. As long as I hung onto the canoe, I didn't have any reason to be worried about having to swim with a dead weight on one foot.

Suddenly, however, something went horribly wrong!

As I looked around, I noticed that Tim had disappeared. He had been right next to me. As I called his name, I realized he was still hanging onto the canoe, but his arms were over his head with his elbows locked straight, causing his head to be underwater. He was a novice swimmer, and he was paralyzed with fear. Vernon and I grabbed him under the armpits and pulled him up.

"Keep your head above water, and you'll be okay!" I shouted to him. But the moment we let go of him, Tim panicked and slipped under the water again.

Vernon and I immediately pulled him back to the surface.

"Grab the thwart! Keep your head above water!" I yelled as I put his hands on the thwart. Al reached across from the other side and grabbed his hands, helping him hang on. We kept encouraging him: "We're going to be okay!" "Hang in there!" "The Lord's going get us out of this."

I managed to grab the lifejacket that had been in our canoe, and Vernon and I tried to put it on Tim. We battled the waves while hanging on to the canoe with one hand and struggling with Tim's lifejacket with the other. But Tim was frozen with fear and wouldn't let us get the lifejacket between the canoe and his chest. Whatever we tried, we simply could not get that lifejacket on him.

"Are you guys okay?" Don called out as he and Bob paddled their canoes up next to us, and we grabbed the gunnels of the closest canoe. We yelled back, "Yeah!"

"Head for the island, Bob!" Don yelled.

"No sir! The shore is our best bet. It's closer, and we'll have the wind and waves at our backs!" Bob protested.

"You're right. Let's go!" Don replied as they headed for the mainland shore.

My brother hung onto Bob's canoe while the rest of us grabbed Don's canoe.

"Don't pull down at all on the canoe or we will swamp!" Don shouted over the storm. "Swim along with us!"

We tried to do as he said, but each wave that came up behind us seemed to splash even more water into the canoe. With four people in the canoe and three of us hanging on its sides, we were in a desperate situation. It wasn't long before one strong wave washed up and over the stern of the canoe, swamping it.

"Bob, come back!" we screamed. "Oh no, what are we going to do? Lord, help us!" We floundered around in the water while hanging onto the canoe with all the strength we had left.

The guys in Bob's canoe looked over their shoulders and saw us, but they didn't stop! Apparently, they decided to head to shore, empty their canoe, and come back to help us. We had been pushed to about three hundred yards from shore by now. The guys in Bob's canoe paddled for shore with every ounce of their being while Jerry bailed water and rolled camping gear into the lake to lighten their load.

Meanwhile, things were deteriorating rapidly for us. When our canoe swamped, the right thing to do would have been to keep our cool, hang onto the canoe, and wait for Bob's canoe to return.

But that's not what happened!

When our canoe swamped, Don and his paddling partner, Kim Graham, stowed their paddles under a thwart between the packs and the side of the canoe to keep them from floating away. Then they, along with Chuck and Dan, climbed out of the canoe so we could hold onto the opposite sides of the submerged canoe to give us a large, stable, and buoyant life preserver. Al had noticed the terror in Tim's eyes, so he grabbed the ski belt from Don's canoe and was trying to get it on Tim when things turned from bad to worse.

Don was talking to us the whole time in a calm voice. "We're going to be all right. All we need to do is hang onto the canoe. Its buoyancy will keep us up. Bob will be back to get us soon."

I heard Don's words, but they didn't sink in.

To this day, I still don't know what made me do what I did next. Maybe it was the wind and the waves that caused me to lose control of my senses. Perhaps it was the fear and terror of suddenly realizing that everything seemed hopeless and that we might die. I just don't know why—but I panicked.

And then I did something very stupid—something I will regret for the rest of my life.

I heard myself saying, "He's right! So let's have some fun!" With that I did the absolutely worst thing I could possibly do in this situation.

I climbed into the swamped canoe and stood up, saluting, as the canoe was being pushed down by my weight below everyone's reach. As the canoe sank, I yelled out, "A captain always goes down with his ship!"

My foolish, inexplicable actions set off a string of events that would end in disaster.

"Miller, don't!" someone yelled.

"Stop it!" cried another.

And, "Duane, what are you doing!?"

The canoe slipped from under my feet, causing me to fall to the right. When the canoe bobbed back to the surface, all of us were on the same side of it. Dan and Al grabbed backpacks and sleeping bags that were floating nearby. Kim was able to take off his hiking boots and swim to shore using a tent bag for floatation. The other four of us grabbed the canoe, but we were all on the same side, causing it to barrel roll and putting us underwater.

Suddenly, Don, Tim, Chuck, and I were desperately fighting for our lives.

The hiking boot I had on felt like a lead weight. I couldn't tread water with it on, and I struggled to swim to the surface. When I made it to the surface, I grabbed the side of the canoe and pulled myself up across it so my head was out of the water and I could breathe. As I began to inhale deeply, the canoe barrel rolled again and a wave hit me in the face, causing me to suck in water and plunging me under the surface. I was terrified. The combination of stress and icy cold water caused my muscles to cramp. This, plus the excruciating pain of the water in my lungs, made me realize that I was drowning. My body wanted to cough and expel the water I had breathed in, but because I was under water, I couldn't. This only intensified the agonizing pain in my chest.

I clawed and fought my way back to the surface a second time. Grabbing the thwart of the canoe, I again pulled myself up and lay across the swamped canoe where I was able to cough hard and inhale once before another wave rolled the canoe. I was still inhaling when I went under and sucked in more water.

I was desperate. With every ounce of strength I had left, I struggled to the surface again. As I broke through the surface and began to inhale, Don shot up out of the water. I saw him gasp for air as water poured off his head. He grabbed for the canoe as it rolled over, plunging both of us under again.

As I sank again into the depths of the lake, I tried to swim to the surface, but all my strength and energy was gone. Indescribable pain wracked my body as every muscle seemed to cramp. The water in my lungs was excruciating.

I knew I was drowning.

At first I was terrified, but then peace washed over me, and I began to relax and sink deeper into the lake. *Is this what it is like to die?* I thought. *Okay, Lord, here I come.*

At that moment I encountered the presence of the Lord in a direct and personal way I never thought possible. There was no bright light or out-of-body experience, just a beautiful, peaceful encounter with the reality that I didn't need to fear death.

The words He spoke to my heart were both kind and understanding, as well as authoritative—like a combination of my mom and my football coach—telling me to get back up to the surface. Instantly, the pain was gone, and I had the strength to swim to the surface.

When I miraculously made it to the surface this time, Al was hanging on to the other side of the canoe to counterbalance it— allowing me to lock my armpits over the canoe's gunnels and hang on for dear life. Dan, who had been hanging onto a sleeping bag for buoyancy, swam over to the canoe and we silently clung onto the canoe together. Words were not necessary; we all knew the gravity of our situation.

I looked toward the shore and noticed that Bob's canoe was already on its way back to help us. When he and Wes arrived several minutes later, it was clear what a dire situation we were in.

Bob noticed that some of the guys were missing and called out in desperation: "Where are the others?"

I looked at Bob and somberly announced, "Captain Don Enzor, Sergeant Chuck Schnittker, and Private Tim Meadows have all gone to be with the Lord."

I don't know how I knew they had drowned. I just knew they were not close to us clutching onto a backpack or sleeping bag, nor could we see then nearby trying to tread water. So I knew they were gone!

I also knew that I was probably the last person to see Don alive.

I was as shocked as anyone with what I heard myself say, but we all knew it was true.

Bob and Wes paddled around our swamped canoe, screaming out their names, looking for any sign of them. After a few minutes, they paddled over to us and had us grab the side of their canoe to take us ashore.

I was still hanging on when I felt the solid rock of the shore under my feet. I let go of the canoe and began to scramble up onto shore. I tried to stand up, but I fell flat on my face. I was shaking so hard and was so exhausted that I had to crawl on my hands and knees, half dragging myself up the hill to the level spot where Jerry had pitched a tent.

Bob and Wes went back out to search more thoroughly.

The five of us who had been in the water—Al, Kim, Dan, Vernon, and me—stumbled, soaking wet, chilled to the bone, and shaking almost uncontrollably into that tiny, three-man pup tent. We were too cold to talk except for the random, "Ouch!" or "Sorry" as we struggled to get out of our wet clothes and an errant elbow or knee hit another guy.

It had been at least forty-five minutes from the time the first canoe swamped until we made it to shore. Those forty-five minutes would dramatically change our lives and the lives of countless people. But at the time, all we knew was that three young men were dead, we were stranded in the wilderness with a storm raging around us, and the rest of our group was on a tiny island about three quarters of a mile away—with no idea what had just happened.

As we sat there in exhaustion and sadness, I recalled hearing Don say that he believed God was going to do something amazing on the trip. What? How? Nothing made sense, and everything seemed hopeless. We had cried out to God for help countless times during our struggles, but He didn't seem to answer.

Where was God in all of this?

CHAPTER FIVE

WHERE WAS GOD?

As our feet hit solid ground of shore, a page was turned and a new chapter began.

Three of our friends lay dead on the bottom of the lake, three canoes were floating just under the surface, eight of us were on shore of the mainland, and the remaining twelve were out on a tiny island offshore. In addition, we were ten miles from the ranger's station. As the rain and wind continued to rage all around us, our situation seemed hopeless.

The moment we made it to the shore of Opeongo Lake, our focus shifted from survival to getting warm. The five of us who scrambled out of the lake were exhausted. Our strength and energy were totally spent. It was all we could do to crawl up the hill and collapse into the tent Jerry had pitched.

As we packed into that three-man pup tent, we resembled a writhing knot of earthworms. Soaking wet and shaking almost uncontrollably, we struggled to get out of our wet clothes. We began to rub each other down to help get blood circulating as we stripped down to our underwear and threw our wet clothes out to Jerry, who wrung them out and put them on sticks by the blazing fire to dry. Very little was said because our teeth were chattering and we were shaking too much.

Besides, after what had just happened with our three friends, what could we possibly say? We were in shock and overwhelmed by the solemnness of the moment.

We began to warm up as the temperature and humidity inside the tent took on the feel of a sauna. With the wind still blowing hard off Opeongo Lake and our clothes not yet dry, we were trapped inside our little cocoon of protection.

Suddenly, Dan started crying and screaming out, "They're dead! They're dead! What are we going to do? How are we going to get out of here? Why didn't God stop it?" His barrage of questions poured out like a flood as his heart burst with the reality of the tragedy.

Even though he was expressing what each of us was feeling, with tears streaming down our own faces, several guys grabbed him and shook him and as we yelled at him to stop. We were scared, shaken, heartbroken, and lost in a wilderness of grief, but it was far too early for us to begin to deal with reality or the questions that accompanied it.

Dan's outburst did get us talking, though. Random thoughts and questions began to pour out, rapid fire, from each of us as we took our first steps toward processing what had happened. Though five voices were speaking, it was as if collectively we were speaking as one.

"Did it really happen?"

"I've never been this scared my whole life!"

"What are we going to do now?"

"I know the Lord is going to get us out of here, but how?"

"But why are we alive and they are dead? Why did God allow us to live? There must be a reason why."

Al spoke up, "Do you realize that three canoes swamped, and one person from each canoe drowned? I don't think that was a coincidence. It seemed like the moment Don, Chuck, and Tim went down, something changed. We weren't struggling anymore, and we all calmed down."

Our conversation was interrupted by Jerry shaking a tent pole,

"Hey, you guys want some food? Unzip the tent so I can hand it in to you."

I was closest to the door, so I unzipped the tent fly enough for Jerry to hand me a hot can of Spam with the lid off and my hunting knife stuck into the side as a pot handle. I pulled the knife out and used it to cut the chunk of Spam into five pieces, which we instantly devoured.

As I put the empty can and my knife on the ground outside the tent door, Kim called out, "That was great Jerry. How 'bout some more?"

The food took a little of the chill from our bodies and gave us a chance to think. Before long, the conversation resumed.

"I can't help but think of how Don liked to quote 'to be absent from the body is to be present with the Lord,'" Dan reminisced.

"I was thinking the same thing," Vernon chimed in. "And I must admit, as scared as I am, I have this sense of peace about those guys. I know that they are with Jesus this very moment, and I feel like the Lord doesn't want us to grieve for them, but for their families and loved ones."

These comments got me thinking, so I joined in, "I remember Don teaching the morning Bible studies at camp from Romans 8:28, 'And we know that all things work together for good to them that love God, to them who are the called according to his purpose' (KJV). I want to see how God works this for good."

Everyone grunted his agreement.

This verse had taken on an entirely new meaning for all of us. It gave us comfort and hope, assuring us that the Lord had not abandoned us.

While we were holed up in the tent, Bob and Wes were paddling around the area where the accident had occurred and checking the nearby shoreline in search of any sign of Don, Chuck, or Tim. After not finding anything related to the three, they went out to the island to tell the rest of the group the terrible news. When they returned, they brought dry clothes and food for those of us packed in the tent.

Some time later, Bob yelled, "A boat is going by the island!" Opeongo Lake is one of the few lakes in Algonquin Park that permits outboard motorboats on its waters. Normally, you only see or hear a handful of boats on Opeongo Lake on any given day. This was the first one we had seen all day. In fact, as we found out later, it was probably the only boat on the lake that day.

We scrambled out of the tent and joined the guys over on the island in waving our arms and rain ponchos while screaming at the top of our voices to try to get the attention of the man in the boat. Unfortunately, the boat passed by the island, continued down the lake and out of sight—taking with it our hopes of being rescued.

The dry clothes and the food helped to cut the chill from being wet and relieve the hunger worked up during our struggle in the water, but we were still numb. We were like animals in a zoo, penned up in a cage with invisible bars, constantly pacing, sitting, and moving about with no real purpose or aim. We continued doing the same thing over and over: one moment sitting in the tent, the next standing by the fire, then walking down to the edge of the water to stare out over the area where Don, Chuck, and Tim lay, only to return to the tent to get away from the chill of the wind, and then repeat the whole process again and again.

We couldn't see it, but the Lord was orchestrating our rescue.

We later learned from the guys who were on the island that the man in the boat had been heading down to the dock at the south end of the lake. He was camping with his wife and their twelve-year-old daughter on the far end of the North Arm of Opeongo Lake. The night before, a black bear had raided their campsite and destroyed their food supply. They had awakened the next morning to find their food gone. But rather than leave, they decided to restock their food. So the man took their boat to the other end of the lake where their car was parked at the access point and drove into the small town of Whitney to get groceries.

When he returned to his boat, he was surprised when a park ranger walked up to him and asked, "Where you headin'?"

"Far end of the North Arm," was his reply.

"I can't let you go up there. The storm's too severe. Only a fool would go there in weather like this," the ranger warned.

"I appreciate your concern, but my wife and daughter are up there with a hungry bear in the area. I'm not going to leave them there alone without food or any way to get away from the bear if it comes back. I know how to handle my boat in these kind of waves."

With these words the man climbed into his boat and headed up the lake toward his family's campsite. That is why he was probably the only boat on Opeongo Lake that day—the only boat on a lake with over 108 miles of shoreline—and why he took a route that went by a tiny island not much bigger than a small house, the very island where our guys were.

Jerry's older brother, Gary, was on the island, and later described the scene there. "About three hours after the man in the boat passed our island, one of the guys scanning the horizon with binoculars shouted, "'Here he comes!'

"Immediately we sprang into action, doing everything we could think of to get his attention—blowing our whistles, waving our arms and rain ponchos, yelling at the top of our voices, even climbing trees and waving orange rain ponchos."

On shore, Bob, Jerry, and Wes also saw the boat, so they stood in a clearing on a hill overlooking the lake and waved an orange tarp and orange ponchos—but to no avail.

Just like before, the man missed everyone's efforts to flag him down, leaving both of our groups hopeless as he continued on.

But then everything changed! Suddenly and inexplicably, the man turned around and spotted the signals for help. He turned his boat around and guided it to the shore of the island.

"We need your help!" Mike shouted. "There's been an accident, and three of our guys are missing. We think they have drowned."

"Jump in!" the man replied. "I'll take you to get help."

Mike and Gary climbed into his boat and went with him to inform the authorities. The man later told our leaders, "I don't know why, but I felt compelled to turn around and look at the island."

When they arrived at the dock at the south end of the lake, Mike and Gary found the rangers and immediately told them what had happened. In an instant, an emergency response plan was put into action—rangers began arriving and boatloads of them began heading up the lake. A floatplane was called in, and it landed at the dock to pick up Gary so he could help guide them to us. Meanwhile, Mike stayed at the dock to begin contacting people back home.

It wasn't long before we heard the sound of a number of boat motors. We scrambled out of the tent and stood in a nearby clearing to watch as a small armada of boats filled with park rangers began to arrive on the North Arm of Opeongo, fanning out across the area where the accident occurred. Some boats crisscrossed the water over the area where the accident had happened, while others landed on the nearby islands and the shore to search for any sign of Don, Chuck, or Tim. It soon became apparent that there was little hope of their survival. The search team's focus transitioned from search and rescue to a recovery mission.

As most of the boats searched for Don, Chuck, and Tim, others were deployed to our campsite. Their arrival shattered the eerie sense of quiet that had enveloped us as we each struggled to process what had happened. As much as we wanted to be rescued, there was something in us that didn't want to leave—that site on the side of the lake had become hallowed ground. Three young men had been ushered into the presence of the Lord near there, and that area of the lake was the door through which they had walked into glory. How could we leave without acknowledging that?

Our reverent, sacred quiet was interrupted by reality. We were being rescued. When the rangers came into our campsite, they immediately took charge. Questions and instructions filled the air:

"Are any of you hurt?"

"How are you holding up?"

"In a minute a boat is going to take you out to the plane, once it lands, so leave everything here. We will bring it back on the boats."

Our campfire was doused, our tent was taken down, and we gathered at the water's edge to await our boat ride to the floatplane.

As the floatplane circled above us, the wind continued to howl and the waves were as choppy as ever—making it impossible for the floatplane to land. However, as it circled, the heavy, dark clouds began to roll back from the west to the east like a huge roll of old, dingy carpeting being rolled up. God was working a miracle right before our eyes! In a matter of minutes, clear blue skies appeared from behind the roll of dark clouds. The wind died down, and the waves calmed enough to allow the floatplane to land.

We were ferried out on the boats to the floatplane, which would fly us to the ranger station at the south end of the lake. We scrambled into the side door of the plane and into the seats. As we finished fastening our seat belts, the door was closed and the plane's engine revved up. Moments later we were airborne. As we flew over the treetops, I looked out my window and whispered to myself, "Wow, this is beautiful! I only wish I could enjoy it."

I was standing near the dock when the third and last planeload of our guys arrived. As Bob and Jerry climbed out of the floatplane on the final trip, they exclaimed, "You won't believe what we just saw! Just as we became airborne, the storm clouds rolled back into place, and we felt the plane buck as the wind blew! The storm picked up right where it left off!"

Was this a coincidence? Absolutely not! There is no doubt in my mind that the Lord was reaching down and wrapping His arms around a bunch of scared guys who were deep in shock over the deaths of three of their friends. What we were experiencing was what theologians call the manifest presence of God. The Lord was making His presence known in very tangible ways.

But this raises a very important question: If God was able to orchestrate the intricate sequence of events that caused there to be one boat on Opeongo Lake to initiate our rescue, and if He could demonstrate His power over creation by having the clouds roll back and the wind die down, then why didn't He do anything to prevent the deaths of Don, Chuck, or Tim? Where was God when they really needed Him?

Up to this point in my life, I believed that life on earth was temporary. In reality, though, I lived as if it wasn't. Being a typical teenager, I thought I was indestructible and that death was something that happened to old people. I treated my salvation in Jesus like a life insurance policy—good to have but not really relevant to everyday life. However, because I had suddenly and shockingly come face to face with mortality—mine and my missing friends'—I was forced to realize that eternity is real. And that now I needed to live life in this reality.

In the months and years that followed, this realization drove me to God's Word in search of answers. I eventually came to the conclusion that God was not surprised by what happened on the lake that day. It didn't catch Him off guard. He wasn't looking down on us and wringing His hands saying, "Why didn't they have lifejackets on? What I am going to do? I wasn't expecting them in heaven yet!"

It was just the opposite. God heard our cries for help, and He was there with us the entire time—even when Don, Chuck, and Tim took their last breaths. Their deaths were not an accident but rather an appointment. It was the time the Lord had set for them to meet Him face to face. David spelled out this concept in the Psalms when he wrote: "All the days ordained for me were written in your book before one of them came to be" (Psalm 139:16 NIV).

This passage, and many others, forced me to realize that before I could gain any understanding of the questions that flooded my mind, I needed to change my perspective. Living life as if this were all there is to it kept me wallowing in self-centered attempts at dead-end answers. My life was not supposed to be about having my needs met, feeling good about myself, or living pain free. Life on this planet is tied directly to eternity. There is more to life than what this planet has to offer.

Later, one of the ways God opened my heart to show me what really happened that day on Opeongo Lake was my love for football. And through that sport he continued to teach me the principle that things never go wrong; they only go different. It is no secret that things in this life may not turn out the way we think they should, but that doesn't mean God doesn't know what He is doing.

Every summer, aspiring football players show up on the first day of pre-season full of energy and dreams of bringing home the championship. Before the first game can be played, though, they must survive preseason. Each day is filled with long, grueling two-a-day practices, hour after hour of conditioning and running drills, exhaustion, frustration, and questioning whether or not it is worth it. Many drop out and quit while others are cut from the team.

Every minute of the preseason practices is intricately planned by the coaching staff to mold a hodge-podge of individuals into a team and to prepare that team for the challenge ahead. For the most part, preseason is a mix of hard work, enjoyment, and a growing sense of accomplishment. However, preseason is not why anyone joins the team. Everyone knows that what really matters is yet to come—the season.

The season gives purpose to the pain and struggle athletes endure in the days leading up to the first game. For each individual, preseason determines three fundamental truths: whether or not they made the team, what position they will play, and whether they are on the starting lineup.

This experience that we call life on planet earth serves similar purposes. This life is not the game; it is simply the preseason for the season called eternity. However, it is vital because what we do in this life determines whether we are on the team of Jesus Christ or on the team of Satan (see Revelation 20:10–15).

Consider what God's Word says about the future of those who have "made the team" by receiving the gift of eternal life through faith in Jesus Christ: "But to all who did receive him, who believed in his name, he gave the right to become children of God" (John 1:12).

And for God's children, they will see "the throne of God and of the Lamb will be in [the city], and his servants will worship him. They will see his face, and his name will be on their foreheads. And night will be no more. They will need no light of lamp or sun, for the Lord God will be their light, and they will reign forever and ever" (Revelation 22:3–5).

The lives of our three friends did not end that fateful day. Rather, on July 21, 1970, Don Enzor, Chuck Schnittker, and Tim Meadows broke into the starting lineup of heaven. Their preseason ended, and they are now living life the way God had intended for it to be lived: in power, indescribable beauty, perfection, and holiness, reigning at the side of Jesus in the kingdom of heaven. What is the eternal season like for them? "No eye has seen, nor ear heard, nor the heart of man imagined, what God has prepared for those who love him" (1 Corinthians 2:9).

Through the years, people have asked me, "Why didn't God intervene and keep this tragedy from happening? He could have done something to prevent all this pain and heartache."

But God isn't in the business of fixing everything. He is not a doting old grandfather, sitting in heaven trying to keep everyone happy and safe. He is the Almighty God who loves us with an everlasting love, and He is causing all things to "work together for good."

One of the reasons He allows pain and suffering to occur is so we can learn to trust Him and his Word. The psalmist described it this way: "If your law had not been my delight, I would have perished in my affliction" (Psalm 119:92).

It is the combination of affliction and the Word of God that transforms us. Pain, suffering, death, disease, and disability are all the consequence of living in a fallen, sinful world. Everyone, whether or not we are followers of Christ, experiences these things as we go through life. But when we allow the Word of God to mold and shape us as we walk through life's challenges—both good and bad—we experience the transforming power of God in our lives.

The Lord did not cause Don, Chuck and Tim to drown just so He could teach us a lesson. Rather, as we experienced one of the tragedies of life, God's Word became a source of strength, guidance, and instruction—helping us to see things from more of an eternal perspective. As the apostle Paul wrote: "All Scripture is breathed out by God and is profitable for teaching, for reproof, for correction, and for training in righteousness, that the man of God may be complete, equipped for every good work" (2 Timothy 3:16–17).

Shortly before His arrest and crucifixion, Jesus spoke these words to His disciples: "Every branch that does bear fruit he prunes, that it may bear more fruit. Already you are clean because of the *word* that I have spoken to you" (John 15:2–3, emphasis added). It is the Word that cleanses or prunes us—that trims out the dead wood and unhealthy things in our lives so we can experience greater growth and fruitfulness.

In football, the pain, exhaustion, and stress of the two-a-day practices were all for a greater purpose. Our coaches wanted to teach us discipline and prepare us for the upcoming season. But it wasn't the affliction of physically being pushed to the limit while wearing helmets and protective gear in the August heat that made a difference. Other people experience the same type of conditions regularly—steel workers, firefighters, soldiers, to name a few, and their difficult experiences have no impact on whether or not they become good football players.

What made the difference were the words our coaches spoke to us while we were going through the drills and difficult times on the practice field. Their knowledge, guidance, and examples—their words—took a ragtag group of teenage boys and molded us into a disciplined, championship team.

We were stronger and more focused as a result of the discipline they had instilled in us. The same is true for God's discipline. "For the moment all discipline seems painful rather than pleasant, but later it yields the peaceful fruit of righteousness to those who have been trained by it" (Hebrews 12:11).

Peter explained trials this way: "In this you rejoice, though now for a little while, if necessary, you have been grieved by various trials, so that the tested genuineness of your faith—more precious than gold that perishes though it is tested by fire—may be found to result in praise and glory and honor at the revelation of Jesus Christ" (1 Peter 1:6–7).

This testing in life develops perseverance—stug, enabling us to keep paddling through whatever storms we face in life. As we do, we experience the power of Christ enabling us to deal with each wave of adversity and pain as it crashes against us. As God's Word tells us in 1 Corinthians 10:13, "No temptation has overtaken you that is not common to man. God is faithful, and he will not let you be tempted beyond your ability, but with the temptation he will also provide the way of escape, that *you may be able to endure it*" (emphasis added).

Everything we were experiencing as a result of the canoeing accident, coupled with God's Word, was teaching us to trust that the Lord knows what He is doing—more than the best coaches in the world. Though at that moment nothing seemed to make sense, we could hold onto the truth of His Word and persevere. He was going to see us through all the turmoil and grief that lay before us, and walk with us to the very end—and what an unbelievable end it is going to be!

CHAPTER SIX

PEACE

When our plane landed at the dock on the south end of Opeongo Lake, we noticed that this once quiet little access point had been transformed into center of activity—people were everywhere. Park Rangers, members of the Ontario Provincial Police, and park staff were scurrying about talking on walkie-talkies, calling out instructions to one another, carrying gear or just trying to look busy. Several ambulances lined up next to the dock with their rear doors open in anticipation with their EMT's standing by. As we climbed out of the plane, we stood in a clump, overwhelmed, not knowing what to do or where to go.

Just then a ranger walked up to us and asked, "Would you gentlemen please follow me?"

Those of us who had been on the shore were taken into the park ranger's office. We each sat down with a separate ranger, who gave us an opportunity to tell our story. When they were finished, most of the guys were allowed to join the rest of the group as they arrived in other planeloads.

When I finished describing everything that had happened, the ranger talking with me asked, "Would you mind staying here for a few minutes so we can get some additional information?"

Soon topographical maps of Opeongo Lake were spread out on a table and the three of us who had been asked to stay were asked to take a look.

"Here is the spot on shore where you were rescued," one of the rangers pointed out, "and here is the island where the rest of your group had been. Do you think you can identify about where the accident occurred? It would help us know where to begin the search."

We silently glanced at each other. We knew that even though he spoke in terms of a search and rescue, what he really meant was the recovery of their bodies.

As I played back the images in my memory and transposed them to the surface of the map, things began to come together for me. I glided my fingers over the map as I talked through what had happened and where.

"This is about where Chuck's canoe was when it swamped," I pointed out. "We would've been about here when we got them out of the water and headed for the island."

Bob pointed to the map, "So we would have been about here when your canoe went down, Miller."

I nodded in agreement.

Suddenly, Kim spoke up, "So that would mean the accident happened about here," as he pointed to a spot on the map. As he did, we all shook our heads in agreement. "That's it!" we exclaimed.

"Let's hope you are right," the ranger responded. "That is on the edge of an underwater cliff where the depth plummets from about fifty feet to about one hundred fifty feet."

"Thanks for your help. You guys can leave now," the ranger in charge said to us as he walked over to the radio. He turned back toward us and spoke to another ranger, "Would you take these young men over to where they can get some hot food?"

With that, he turned back to the radio and called the rangers who were at the site of the accident and gave them the coordinates for the spot that we had pointed out.

We were led from the rangers' office to another building where a hot meal was being prepared. We hadn't realized how hungry we were until we started to eat. I don't recall what we ate—just that it was warm, good, and there was plenty of it. And it sure hit the spot.

With bellies full, we drifted away from the dining hall. Those of us who were wearing borrowed clothes retrieved our clothes from the cars and changed. Not long after that, a mountain of camping gear and personal belongings began to build on the dock as boat after boat returned from the site of the accident. The rangers had gathered all our gear from the island and our campsite, fished it from the lake, and retrieved it from the shoreline where some of it had floated.

As we began to sift through the pile of waterlogged gear, retrieving what belonged to us, we would come to items belonging to one of our three missing friends. Seeing these things was bad enough, but picking them up to move them was like a slap in the face with reality.

What surprised us about all the gear was that even though we had left everything either on shore or in the middle of the lake, everything was recovered. Even the rain poncho I had ditched when I first went into the water was found. The only personal items I lost were the hiking boot (I had kicked it off when my canoe first swamped) and my hunting knife—which I inadvertently left where the pile of gear had been.

Finally, we were allowed to leave. We loaded the cars and headed into Huntsville to spend the night. Normally, the trip into Huntsville at the end a canoe trip would be a joyous celebration of a great wilderness experience.

This time it was anything but joyous. As Opeongo Lake disappeared behind us, we were left with just our jumbled thoughts and memories. Numbness from shock and grief filled our beings; yet there was an unexplainable sense of peace enveloping us. We silently stared out the car windows at the sights that only a few days earlier had brought excitement and anticipation, but now served as reminders of our loss. Yet the rugged beauty that we passed also stood in silent testimony of God's presence and comfort.

Arrangements were made for us to stay at a hotel in Huntsville. As soon as we were settled in our room, Vernon and I knew we needed to call home and let our family know what had happened. The families of Don, Chuck, and Tim had already been contacted, so we knew that word was beginning to spread. Local radio had already begun to announce the accident, so it was important that our family hear from us. We needed to hear their voices too.

We weren't the only ones who wanted to call home. Once we had made our way down to the hotel lobby, we were greeted by a long line of guys behind the only pay phone in the hotel. We took our place in line and began to wait. Finally, it was our turn to call. As I waited for the operator to complete the collect call to our home, it hit me: what do I say? How was I going to tell my family we were okay but our cousin was dead?

Our parents and younger brother, Roger, were on vacation at our aunt's in Connecticut while our older brother, David, was running the family farm. Our Aunt Grace, who lived in the front half of our house with our cousin Beth, answered the phone.

It was Tuesday. No one was supposed to hear from us until Friday, so the moment she heard the operator say, "Collect call from Duane in Huntsville, Canada," she knew something was wrong.

"Duane, is everything all right?"

"Aunt Grace," I responded, "Vernon and I are okay, but there has been an accident. Chuck, Don Enzor, the director of the camp, and a kid in my canoe, Tim Meadows, drowned."

I can still hear the sorrow in her voice and the breaking of her heart as she replied, "Oh, Duane, I'm so sorry! What happened?"

I continued on and briefly told her the story. It was a relatively short conversation. She asked a few questions, mostly about the welfare of Vernon and me, and when we expected to be home.

"Duane, I'll let your mom and dad know right away. I'm glad you and Vernon are okay, but I'm so sorry about Chuck ..." her voice trailing off as she began to cry. "We will be praying," she said through her tears.

"Thank you," I whispered.

As I silently hung up the phone, I felt as if a huge burden had been lifted. Her quiet calm voice was just what I needed to hear. Aunt Grace was going to make the heart-wrenching call to my parents, and she was going to be praying. I knew that as soon as my parents heard the news they would be on their knees praying as well.

For as long as I could remember, prayer had been an anchor in my family's life. Every day started with a family prayer time. When I was a boy, if I woke up early and went to my grandma's kitchen, I would not only be fed a hot breakfast, but I would also often find Grandma, Aunt Grace, and my dad, Pap, praying together before Grace headed off to work and Pap made his way out to the barn to do chores.

As soon as Pap finished chores, he would come into the house so he could pray with mom, my brothers, and me. Often we would still be eating breakfast when we heard him come in the house. His arrival meant we only had moments to scarf down our half full bowl of cereal before he sat down and simply said, "Okay, let's pray." When he prayed, he prayed for everyone and everything. If there was a need in the neighborhood or family or at church, he prayed for it. Time didn't matter to Pap when he was talking with the Lord. More than once he would be praying and we would hear the school bus honking its horn for us, and he would just keep on praying. Talking with his heavenly Father was more important than our getting to school on time.

When Grace told me that she was going to be praying, I knew they all were going to be kneeling before Jesus and pouring their hearts out to Him, seeking His guidance, strength, and comfort. It wasn't their prayers that made a difference, but who they were praying to. They would be crying out to their Lord and Savior, Jesus, knowing He heard their pleas and feeling His arms around them.

❈

As the word spread about the deaths of Don, Chuck, and Tim, it was prayers like these of countless godly people that the Lord worked through to strengthen and comfort us in our shock and grief. As people prayed, we experienced the "peace of God, which surpasses all understanding" (Philippians 4:7) in tangible ways.

Our hearts ached with the overwhelming agony of having people we loved dearly ripped from our lives. Where just a few hours earlier these men had occupied a place in our lives, there was now a gaping hole in our hearts. It was a wound so big that it threatened to suck us into its abyss of pain.

In the midst of all this indescribable agony and turmoil, the peace of God began to flow over us. God had not abandoned us, and He was sovereign in this entire situation.

He was bringing hope and a future to Don's wife, Twila, who found out two weeks later that she was pregnant with their first child, Aaron.

He was bringing healing and salvation to Tim's family.

He was beginning to make something beautiful out of the devastation in Chuck's family.

None of us knew how and it was too early to see evidences of it, but deep within our hearts we knew that the Lord was taking care of things. That is how the peace of God works—giving strength, comfort, and assurance when nothing seems to make sense and the pain is overwhelming.

CHAPTER SEVEN

HEARTBREAK

The Schnittker house in Chicago Heights, Illinois, was a hubbub of activity the afternoon of July 21. Their backyard was filled with laughing and giggling girls helping Chuck's younger sister, Jan, celebrate her tenth birthday.

Since my cousin Chuck was the fourth child in a family of six kids, constant activity, craziness, and extra kids were nothing unusual around the Schnittker home. As I learned later from Dirk, Chuck's younger brother, he and his friend John Bardis, were "helping" his parents that day by running the games for Jan and her friends—meaning, like any fourteen-year-old boys, they were simply teasing and antagonizing the girls while his parents prepared the food and cake.

Paul, an older brother, had just come home from working a full day as a carpenter's apprentice. As he was walking up the steps of their raised ranch home and heading toward the kitchen to grab a snack, the phone rang. With the party going on, no one thought anything of it—it probably was another grandmother or aunt calling to wish Jan happy birthday.

Chuck's dad, my Uncle Bill, answered the phone. Chet Weigle, a friend of his from Trail to Life Camp, was calling with the horrendous news of the canoeing accident.

"I need it quiet!" Uncle Bill shouted, as the room instantly became silent. "Please say that again … Okay, I understand …"

He turned and spoke. "Paul," he said, "go get Dirk and Jan and have them come in here right away, but ask John to keep everyone else in the backyard." Then he looked at his wife and said, "Mim, come with me."

He and Aunt Mim walked down the hallway and into their bedroom, closing the door behind them. In a few moments, a heart-wrenching wail went through the house, "NO! Lord, please no!" as the sounds of a mother's heart breaking was heard by all.

A couple of minutes later, Uncle Bill and Aunt Mim walked out of their room holding each other, tears streaming down their faces. They sat down at the kitchen table and gave Dirk, Jan, and Paul the news: Chuck, along with Don and Tim, was missing in the wilderness of Canada and presumed dead. Uncle Bill told them that nothing was definitive as the search for them was ongoing.

Friends who lived nearby walked home while the rest piled into the car, and Paul drove them home. No one knew whether to grieve or pray for a miracle. The heartache and fear that Chuck might be dead mixed with the hope that until his body was recovered he might still be alive. This created a cocktail of confusion. The uncertainty of it all made Chuck's absence even more difficult.

News of Chuck's disappearance spread like wildfire as the kids arrived home from the birthday party. Adding to the impact was the fact that Chuck had babysat many of the girls who were at the party. As a result, the phone started ringing off the hook and friends began arriving to lend support. In the midst of all the confusion, Bill and Mim's concern was getting the news of the tragedy to their older children. Chuck's older sister, Sandy, a newlywed, had just moved to upstate New York with her husband. The old house they had purchased didn't have phone service. Fortunately, her in-laws lived about thirty minutes away.

Al, Chuck's oldest brother, was serving with the Army in

Vietnam. Phone calls to the Army Recruiting Office and the Red Cross got the ball rolling to make emergency contact with him, but it was his Battalion Commander's personal intervention that enabled Al to be home within forty-eight hours.

The moment the phone rang, the Schnittkers discovered that there is no playbook for dealing with family devastation—no instruction manual they could consult about how to respond. There was so much going on that was totally out of their control, yet they felt they should be doing something—anything to make the growing pain go away.

Aunt Mim began to wander around in shock, trying to clean up the party mess, but not accomplishing anything—putting things away in the wrong place, picking up used paper plates and cups, only to set them down in a random location.

Uncle Bill was like a caged tiger. He paced around the house and yard, lost in his thoughts. Shortly after the kids from the party were gone, he announced, "I just can't sit here. I need to be there. I'm going to Algonquin Park to find out for myself what is happening." With that, he turned and walked into his bedroom and began to throw some clothes into a suitcase.

Soon after Paul had returned from taking the kids home, his dad walked out of the bedroom with his suitcase in hand. He embraced Aunt Mim, and they wept together. Stepping back, he quietly said, "I don't mean to leave you here at such a terrible moment, but that's our son that's missing and I feel so helpless. I've got to be there to see if there is anything I can do. I will call you."

"I understand. I will be praying," Aunt Mim quietly responded.

They embraced and kissed, and Uncle Bill picked up his suitcase and headed for the door. Turning to Paul, he said, "Grab your shoes, I need you to come with me to the airport so you can bring the car home."

Uncle Bill was heading out of the house to his car when Pastor William Gaskell pulled into the driveway. Pastor Gaskell was the pastor of Village Bible Church in Park Forest, Illinois, where the Schnittkers attended. When Pastor Gaskell had received the news, he dropped everything and rushed over to the Schnittker home.

Pastor Gaskell was an outgoing, loving pastor who was a strong Bible preacher. He had recognized the potential in Chuck and took him under his wing to disciple him.

As Pastor Gaskell walked up to Uncle Bill in the driveway that afternoon, he asked, "Bill where are you going?"

"I'm heading to the airport. I need to get to Algonquin Park to find out for myself what is going on," Uncle Bill replied.

"You're not going alone, Bill, I'm going with you," Pastor Gaskell instructed, "But let's go back inside so I can call my wife and let her know what is going on."

The two men turned and walked into the house. When they had walked up the steps into the living room, Pastor Gaskell asked everyone to sit down so they could talk.

"Tell me what you know about what has happened," he inquired.

Uncle Bill then recounted to him everything that he had been told by Chet on the phone.

Pastor Gaskell then spoke words that the family remembers to this day, "With the Lord, there are never accidents, only incidents that draw us closer to Him."

They then began to reminisce about Chuck and the impact he had on so many people, as well as rejoicing, even in the midst of their heartbreak, of the assurance that Chuck, Don, and Tim were at that very moment enjoying the indescribable joys of heaven. Memory after memory began to flow about Chuck. At times they were laughing about one of Chuck's crazy antics, and then a moment later, weeping together over their heartbreak. Chuck was a very special and unique teenager.

Anyone who knew Chuck when he was a kid knew that he was a ticking time bomb. He was smart, athletic, and arrogant. Even as a young boy, he lived as if life was all about him. If he happened to fail or someone beat him at something, he would explode into a rage. More than once I had to run for my life because he had lost it and threw punches or was swinging a baseball bat or garden hoe at whomever was around.

Chuck received Jesus as his Savior when he was nine and attending TTLC for the first time. Several years later, at age fourteen, he dedicated his life to Christ. It was evident that something had changed in him. This was so much more than an emotional or religious experience. He sold out totally to Jesus.

The first thing he did when he came home from TTLC that year was to find a Bible teaching church to attend. The family had been attending another church, but Chuck had never heard the message of salvation or of surrendering his life to Christ taught there, so he set out to find a church that was all about Jesus. He found that church in Village Bible Church in Park Forest. Soon the entire Schnittker family was attending.

His hunger for God's Word and prayer transformed his life. Many mornings his brothers Paul and Dirk would be awakened at 4:30 by the dim light of the desk in their room. They'd roll over to see Chuck sitting there studying the Bible or praying before he headed out to do his daily paper route at 5:30.

This new love for Jesus also spilled over into a love for people. He wanted everybody he knew to know Christ, so he set out to tell them. Where pride and arrogance once ruled, humility reigned supreme. Peace and joy had replaced temper and rage. Caring and compassion flowed from his life. Chuck was still competitive and always played to win, but he now knew that there were more important things in life than winning. He had been set free from the bondage of pride and rage and wanted to tell people about it, so witnessing about Jesus became a normal part of his everyday conversations.

He took a lot of flak and persecution at first from his friends and teammates, but that didn't dampen his spirit. By the time he was a junior in high school, the hassling had subsided. A combination of respect for his athletic accomplishments in football, wrestling, and track plus the authenticity of his character and walk with the Lord silenced those who mocked him.

It was evident that Galatians 2:20 was his life verse: "I have been crucified with Christ. It is no longer I who live, but Christ lives in me. And the life I now live in the flesh, I live by faith in the Son of God."

The more the family reminisced about Chuck, the more they felt their feet coming back under them, enabling them to stand on the Rock of Jesus Christ against the storm of grief that had struck their home.

Pastor Gaskell then spoke up, "Let's spend some time talking to the Lord."

With that, they bowed their heads and poured their hearts out, expressing their grief and heartbreak, thanking God for allowing Chuck to be a part of their lives, and praising God for the fact that they could grieve with hope—the hope and assurance that Chuck was in the presence of God at that very moment. They also asked that the eyes of their hearts would be opened to what the Lord was doing and know how to respond.

It was during that time that Aunt Mim prayed, "Lord, please pull them from the water." She later explained to me that she knew in her heart that Chuck, Don, and Tim were dead and that "God only wanted their souls, not their bodies." She was praying that their bodies would be recovered quickly.

When they finished praying, it was evident that Uncle Bill was ready to leave. So after Pastor Gaskell called his wife and his secretary to let them know where he was going, the two men jumped in the car and headed to the airport. Paul rode along with them to bring the car home. No one had ever accused Uncle Bill of driving too slow—that day was no exception. Pastor Gaskell hung on, white knuckled, as Uncle Bill made it to the airport in what had to be record time. After Uncle Bill and Pastor Gaskell flew from

Chicago to Toronto, they rented a car and drove through the night to Huntsville.

Years later Uncle Bill, Aunt Mim, and I were talking about that trip, and they both said that it made them shudder to think what might have happened if Pastor Gaskell had not gone along. Would he have been able to be strong enough to face what lay ahead? Would he have slid back into old habits? At the time, Uncle Bill was just starting his journey back to Christ.

He had received Jesus as his Savior as a child and had been active in church through his teen years. But while serving in the Navy during World War II, he began to drift from the Lord and picked up the habits of drinking and chain-smoking. As the years progressed, he started abusing alcohol. In time, alcohol took the place of his relationship with Christ. He never denied his faith. He just started to turn to the bottle for help rather than to the Lord.

Uncle Bill was one of the friendliest and most fun-loving people you could ever meet. He was the uncle who would bring the "Whoopee Cushion" to the family Christmas dinner at Grandma's house, and often, when he mispronounced a word would say something like, "I got my tongue caught on my eye tooth and couldn't see what I was saying."

But when he would drink, the alcohol would bring the worst out in him. He would become loud and abusive. It reached the point that just three months before the accident, Aunt Mim gave him an ultimatum—either stop drinking, or she and the kids were leaving. One thing Uncle Bill knew for sure was that he loved his wife and kids, so he quit drinking. He had been completely sober for three months before the accident occurred.

As Uncle Bill and Pastor Gaskell made their journey to Huntsville, they had plenty of time to talk, but few words were said. It was Pastor Gaskell's presence that spoke to Uncle Bill more than words ever could. This time together helped prepare Uncle Bill for the horrendous ordeal that lay ahead.

CHAPTER EIGHT

FULL DISCLOSURE

The morning after the accident, we all awoke early from a fitful night's sleep to the realization that this wasn't just a terrible dream. We were living the nightmare and the accident was reality.

We were half asleep when a leader knocked on our door and called out, "Time to get up. We're meeting downstairs in twenty minutes."

Slowly we rolled out of bed, got dressed, grabbed our tooth-brushes, and numbly shuffled down the hall to join the line outside the small public bathroom on our floor. About half an hour later we were all assembled in the hotel lobby with our personal gear in tow. Just as we finished a short time of prayer and started heading out to the cars to get breakfast, Uncle Bill and Pastor Gaskell walked into the lobby.

When they walked in, everyone stopped and stared, but it seemed right that they were there. They talked a few minutes with a couple of our leaders and then walked over to Vernon and me. "Can we give you two a ride to the restaurant?" Uncle Bill asked.

As Vernon and I climbed into the backseat of their rental car, Uncle Bill turned in his seat so he could face us and asked, "Are you guys okay?"

We assured him we were.

He then asked, "Could you please tell me what happened out there? I need to know everything."

Pastor Gaskell drove the short distance to the restaurant as Vernon and I recounted everything that had happened the day before on Opeongo Lake. Pastor Gaskell parked the car on the street in front of the restaurant and also turned so he could see us as we continued to share the details of the accident. We left nothing out of the story. They had a lot of questions, and we tried our best to answer them.

"Why did you guys have such bad canoes?"

"Why wasn't anyone wearing lifejackets?"

"How did so many of you end up hanging onto Don's canoe?"

"What set off the chain of events at the end?"

There was no finger pointing or even a hint of blame directed at anyone. They simply wanted the facts.

It was heartbreaking to sit in the backseat of that car and describe step by step every detail of the accident. Watching the heart of a man I loved and respected break before my eyes was one of the most difficult things I have ever experienced. But in the midst of the heartbreak, I witnessed a strength begin to emerge from Uncle Bill. He was experiencing the reality of the power of God being "made perfect in weakness" (2 Corinthians 12:9).

The crisis that Uncle Bill was experiencing was a crisis of the soul. His time with Pastor Gaskell brought him face to face with the reality that he had been holding out on God. He was starting to see that he had viewed his salvation as something that was good to have in case he died, but he hadn't allowed it to really make much difference in this life. Now he understood that salvation was a relationship with the Almighty God who loved him with an infinite love. The only logical response to this sacrificial love of God was total surrender to Christ. Jesus had given His all in payment for sin, so it only made sense for Uncle Bill to give his all to Jesus. So he did.

The depth of this new relationship with Christ is what gave Uncle Bill the strength he needed in the midst of crushing grief and sorrow.

He was experiencing the manifest presence of God at a time when he needed it the most. He was also beginning to understand what it was that had so radically changed his son several years earlier when Chuck surrendered his life to Christ.

When Vernon and I finished telling our account of the canoeing accident and answering their questions, Pastor Gaskell asked Vernon and me to put our hands on the back of the front seat. Placing his right hand on top of ours and his left hand on Uncle Bill's shoulder, he began to pray. He prayed for God to make himself known to us in tangible ways. He prayed that the peace of God would flow over us. He prayed that we would know the strength of God in the midst of our weakness. As he prayed, I felt a huge weight being lifted from my heart as the Lord used the words of Pastor Gaskell to once again assure us that we weren't going through this alone.

When he finished praying, we climbed out of the car and headed into the diner as the two men drove away.

While we ate our breakfast, Mike called the ranger office in Algonquin to get an update on the status of the search. Nothing had changed, so after finishing our meal we piled into the cars and started the trip home.

That ride home was the longest ride of my life. It seemed to be ten times longer than the trip to Algonquin had been. Since Don had been our driver and Tim had also been in our car, changes were made in who rode in each car. One of the other adult leaders, Howie Reinhold, became our driver and another teen moved to our car.

For the most part, the trip was spent looking blankly out the window. There was no joking around or kidding each other like there had been on the way up. Once in a while someone would make a comment, but they were simply thinking out loud. Howie occasionally gave us words of comfort and quoted timely Bible verses. Nothing specific he said really made much difference, except to be a voice of comfort. I remember thinking how thankful I was that he was our driver. He was a good friend and he too was heartbroken, but the faith and wisdom that he expressed gave us a rock to stand on.

While we drove home, Uncle Bill and Pastor Gaskell continued on to Algonquin Provincial Park and the ranger station at Opeongo Lake. When Uncle Bill and Pastor Gaskell arrived, a flurry of activity welcomed them. Recovery divers were in the process of loading their equipment into boats. Soon, a string of boats was headed up the lake to the north arm of Opeongo to resume the search.

Uncle Bill and Pastor Gaskell made themselves known to the rangers as soon as they arrived. They were invited into the ranger's station and given a briefing of the situation. Everyone was very helpful and compassionate, but once they were given all the information, a bubble of awkward silence enveloped them. What do you say to a parent who is waiting for divers to recover the body of his son from the bottom of a lake?

Time seemed to drag on for them as they wandered aimlessly around the dock and the various buildings, lost in the fog of heartbreaking uncertainty. Sometimes mingling amongst the people, other times seeking solitude at the water's edge to cry out to God. They would often drift into the rangers' office under the guise of getting another cup of coffee but really hoping to hear something.

Several hours passed and Uncle Bill and Pastor Gaskell happened to be in the ranger station when a call came over the radio:

"Base, we have located a body and are in the process of bringing it to the surface."

"Roger that. Is there any sign of the other two men who are missing?"

"None yet," was the reply.

Those words froze Uncle Bill to the floor. He couldn't move because of the weight of heartbreak that was overwhelming him. He stood motionless, staring out the window, hoping against hope that somehow, someway, the other two guys would be found alive, somewhere on shore.

About half an hour later, Uncle Bill and Pastor Gaskell had just walked back into the rangers' office to check on the status of things when the radio again cracked to life.

"Base, we have located the other two victims and are bringing their bodies to the surface."

"Roger that, we'll see you when you get here."

Even though it was the news they expected, it still felt like a sucker punch.

It was true. His son Chuck was dead.

Pastor Gaskell nodded to the ranger and walked out of the office in silence with Uncle Bill. They walked down to the edge of the water, embraced one another, and wept a flood of tears that only comes from the depth of a shattered soul. Overwhelmed by heart-wrenching agony, Uncle Bill wailed a wail that was beyond words. Together, they slumped to their knees and cried out to the Lord for help.

It was early afternoon and the wind had begun to die down when everyone seemed to stop and look toward the growing sound of boat motors coming around the final bend in the lake. Within minutes the solemn procession of boats arrived at the dock carrying the bodies of Don Enzor, Chuck Schnittker, and Tim Meadows. As they pulled up to the dock, a silence fell over the crowd of officials, reporters, and onlookers gathered there.

The bodies were taken off the boats and transferred to ambulances that had been awaiting their arrival. Uncle Bill and Pastor Gaskell stood on the dock watching the process. Once the bodies were in the ambulances, a ranger approached Uncle Bill.

"Are you sure you still want to do this?" he asked.

Uncle Bill shook his head and whispered, "Yes."

"Okay. Then please follow me," the ranger said as he turned and walked toward the ambulances.

One by one, each body bag was unzipped, and my uncle faced the horrendous task of looking at the pale, lifeless faces of these three young men in their raw condition. With tears streaming down his face, Uncle Bill quietly identified each young man.

As each body bag was opened, it became clear to my uncle that he was not identifying Don, Chuck, or Tim, but the empty shells they once inhabited. As he told me later, Uncle Bill realized each lifeless body was not a symbol of an ending but a beginning. He knew Don, Chuck, and Tim were more alive at that instant than ever before. The encouragement of the Scriptures became reality: "to be absent from the body, and to be present with the Lord" (2 Corinthians 5:8 KJV), and "For me to live is Christ, and to die is gain" (Philippians 1.21). This was the true reality of this accident. Each young man was experiencing life without pain, threat, or need. They were living in the presence of Almighty God and enjoying their relationship with Him.

This knowledge gave my uncle the strength to identify the bodies, talk with the people that had the authority to release the bodies to be sent back to the United States, and to sign all necessary paper work.

In the midst of his own grief and heartbreak, Uncle Bill was able to do what needed to be done because he was beginning to see things from an eternal perspective. He understood that for Don, Chuck, and Tim, their eternal life began the moment they received Jesus as their Savior. Preseason was over. They were in the game and enjoying eternity in heaven. Even in the midst of the most heart-wrenching grief, Uncle Bill received hope and peace. He received the ability to grieve with hope, just as the Bible promises: "But we do not want you to be uniformed, brothers, about those who are asleep, that you may not grieve as others do who have no hope" (1 Thessalonians 4:13).

CHAPTER NINE

JOY

They had identified the bodies of Don, Chuck, and Tim, and the ambulances carrying their remains had just left the dock area of Opeongo Lake. Numb, Uncle Bill and Pastor Gaskell stood staring out over the water trying to grasp the gravity of the situation. Just then, one of the recovery divers walked over and introduced himself.

"I'm glad you are here because I feel there is something you need to know about the recovery of your son's body." He paused for a moment and looked down at the ground shuffling his feet, unsure of how to put into words what he wanted to say. Finally, he looked up at the two men and spoke,

"I have been a recovery diver for many years, and I have lost count of how many bodies I have helped pull out of lakes, rivers, and ponds. In fact, our team came here this morning directly from Toronto where yesterday we had to recover seven bodies from a boating accident in Lake Ontario."

He took a deep breath and continued, "But what I saw today in recovering these bodies I have never witnessed before. Whenever someone is drowning, they are frantically fighting with every ounce of their being to stay alive. So when I find the body of a recent drowning victim underwater, they always have an expression of sheer terror on their face.

"I was the one who found Don's and Chuck's bodies in about fifty feet of water lying next to each other. Another diver found Tim's body about fifty feet away from them. I haven't had a chance to talk with that diver about how he found Tim's body, so I don't know any details about the discovery of Tim."

The diver paused, took another deep breath and looked straight into the eyes of Uncle Bill, as if looking for an answer for what he was about to say, and said, "I found your son lying next to Don Enzor. Both were on their backs with their eyes wide open. However, there was no look of fear or terror in either of their eyes. Instead, they lay with their arms outstretched and an expression on their faces that I can only describe as overwhelming joy! They looked alive, as if they were overcome with happiness. They looked like they were welcoming a really good friend they hadn't seen in a long time."

Tears were welling up in the diver's eyes as he again looked down at the ground and shook his head in confusion, not knowing what to think or say.

Uncle Bill and Pastor Gaskell were speechless. They threw their arms around the diver and wept tears of joy mixed with heartbreak.

A few moments later Uncle Bill and Pastor Gaskell stepped back as Pastor Gaskell spoke: "I believe that what you saw was visible confirmation of a truth of the Bible. All three of the young men that drowned were followers of Jesus. The Bible tells us that the moment a believer dies, they are immediately in the presence of Jesus."

"What you saw," Pastor Gaskell continued, as he locked eyes with the diver, "was the residual effects of the inexpressible joy that Don, Chuck, and Tim experienced when they literally saw Jesus face to face."

Before turning to go back to the dock to help the rest of the team load their gear so they could head out, the diver looked at Uncle Bill and Pastor Gaskell and said, "I've been doing this job for so many years that I have become hardened to the sight of death. I am good at what I do and I feel I am helping to bring closure to grieving families. But all I ever see is death and hopelessness.

"What I saw today has shaken me out of my numbness to death and is making me take a hard look at my own life. When my time comes to die, will I face death in fear and terror, or will it be a joyful experience for me?"

With those words the diver thanked Uncle Bill and Pastor Gaskell, turned, and walked over to the rest of the dive team on the dock. In no time, the dock area was quiet with just a few rangers and other workers milling around.

Amidst their grief and sorrow, Uncle Bill and Pastor Gaskell stood at the water's edge enveloped in an invisible cloud of awe and wonder. God the Father had reached down and picked them up, holding them close to His chest, allowing the sound of His heartbeat to comfort them and bind their broken hearts. He was their source of strength and protection during the horrendous storm they were weathering. In very concrete ways, they were experiencing the fulfillment of the promises of the Bible: "Be merciful to me, O God, be merciful to me, for in you my soul takes refuge; in the shadow of your wings I will take refuge, till the storms of destruction pass by. I cry out to God Most High, to God who fulfills his purpose for me" (Psalm 57:1–2).

"Blessed be the God and Father of our Lord Jesus Christ, the Father of mercies and God of all comfort, who comforts us in all our affliction" (2 Corinthians 1:3–4).

On July 21, 1970, Don Enzor, Chuck Schnittker, and Tim Meadows went swimming with Jesus in Opeongo Lake and then went home with Him, but they didn't bother telling us where they were going! Fortunately, Jesus left us a note telling us where they were:

Let not your hearts be troubled. Believe in God; believe also in me. In my Father's house are many rooms. If it were not so, would I have told you that I go to prepare a place for you? And if I go and prepare a place for you, I will come again and will take you to myself, that where I am you may be also (John 14:1–3).

The assurance of salvation and eternal life is not the result of positive thinking, blind faith, or sincerity of beliefs. A person can have totally wrong thinking, have faith in the wrong thing, or be sincere in believing a dead end. Assurance comes from trusting in what is true and trustworthy. It's more than just having faith; one must have faith in the right thing—salvation in Jesus Christ. "Whoever has the Son has life; whoever does not have the Son of God does not have life. I write these things to you who believe in the name of the Son of God that you may know that you have eternal life" (1 John 5:12–13).

Those who loved Don, Chuck, and Tim were able to grieve with hope knowing that they had eternal life. These verses don't say that Don, Chuck, and Tim *thought* they might have eternal life or *hoped* they were good enough to get it. It says, "that you may *know* that you have eternal life." This knowledge is the basis for confidence in the saving work of Jesus. This knowledge is the foundation for all hope, joy, and peace. The diver's account was simply tangible confirmation of the Bible's promises as truth—encouraging Uncle Bill and Pastor Gaskell to grieve with hope.

God was answering the prayers Uncle Bill, Aunt Mim, and the rest of the family and friends had prayed the day before at the Schnittker home in ways that far exceeded anything they could hope for. Their loved ones were dead, and their hearts felt like they had been ripped out and stomped in the mud. They needed comfort and hope, and God enveloped them in it in an expected way.

As I look back on that day, I can see how the Lord began to teach me an important principle about prayer and how He answers it.

Through the years, I have read many books and heard countless sermons about prayer that say God's answers to our prayers are always, "Yes, No, or Wait." Is that really what the Bible teaches? I have come to realize that this conclusion is overly simplistic and tends to look at things from an earthly rather than an eternal perspective.

Do these words of the apostle Paul sound like Jesus is saying "No" or "Wait"? "Now to Him who is able to do far more abundantly beyond all that we ask or think, according to the power that is at work within us ..." (Ephesians 3:20 NASB).

The Lord's answer to the prayers of His children is always, "Trust Me." Think about it. How often has the Lord's answer to a prayer seemed at first to be a no, but as time passes, you realize that even though His answer was painful, it really was a yes. I don't know how many times I have heard people say that as they look back, they are so thankful that the Lord didn't answer their prayers the way they had hoped. In many cases people say that losing a job, or not getting into the college they had hoped, or experiencing a debilitating illness or injury turned out to be the best thing that could have happened to them. They go on to say that what they learned about the Lord and the richness and depth of their relationship with Him now more than makes up for any pain or suffering that they went through. They now know what it means to trust Him.

Prayer is all about our relationship with the Lord. It is an opportunity to experience the intimacy of the love relationship we have with God through our faith in Jesus. He truly knows what is best for us in light of eternity. He knows how dangerous the trap can be for us to trust in the answers we want. If not getting what we prayed for causes us to turn our back on God, then we were trusting in the answer we wanted rather than trusting in God and His perfect will.

When Jesus taught us how to pray, He said this: "Your Father knows what you need before you ask him. Pray then like this: Our Father in heaven, hallowed be your name. Your kingdom come, your will be done, on earth as it is in heaven. Give us this day our daily bread" (Matthew 6:8–11). When we focus on the Lord and His glory as we pray for the advancement of His kingdom and the fulfillment of His will in our lives and situations, we can confidently lay before Him our specific requests and desires (our daily bread). He is fully aware of our needs even before we are.

God loves us with a pure, holy, infinite, and eternal love. How He demonstrates that love through prayer is seen and understood from the perspective of eternity. "For my thoughts are not your thoughts, neither are your ways my ways, declares the LORD. For as the heavens are higher than the earth, so are my ways higher than your ways and my thoughts than your thoughts" (Isaiah 55:8–9)

When Aunt Mim first heard the news of Chuck's death and prayed, "Lord, please pull them from the water," did God answer her prayer with a simple "yes, no, or wait"? No. He far exceeded anything she could have ever imagined, and her faith and trust in Him was deepened. The Lord used what could have been a routine recovery dive to bring a healing touch to people whose hearts were broken.

In the years that followed the accident, whenever I visited Uncle Bill and Aunt Mim, invariably the conversation flowed to the canoeing accident. Without fail, Uncle Bill always retold the details of what happened on the dock on Opeongo Lake that day. I can still see his eyes mist up and the joyful smile that crept across his face, as he started, "Have I ever told you about my conversation with the diver that discovered Chuck's and Don's bodies?"

Though I had heard it many times before, I always let him continue. Before long my eyes are misting up, and I am smiling along with him.

CHAPTER TEN

DECEIVED

"IT WAS NOT MY FAULT!"

I turned and stormed out of the room, bolted up the steps to my bedroom, and for the first time I cried about what had happened on Opeongo Lake. The tears were not tears of grief or sorrow but of fear and wounded pride.

My parents had just arrived home from Connecticut. No sooner had they walked in the house than Vernon and I sat down with them at our dining table and began telling them the details of the canoeing accident. Our parents sat quietly, listening through their tears to the entire story. When we finished, they started asking questions to gain a better understanding of all that had occurred.

"Why were there only two people in Don's canoe?"

"Why didn't more canoes come back to help?"

"When you saw how bad the waves were, why didn't you put your lifejackets on?"

When I explained that we only had one lifejacket per canoe—and that was only for us to use as padding on the shoulders for the person carrying the canoe on portages—Pap became agitated. Suddenly, he raised his voice and yelled at me, "You mean to tell me that none of you were wearing lifejackets—that there weren't lifejackets for everyone? You know better than that! How could you ever allow this to happen?"

His words were a knife piercing my heart, but I wasn't going to take the blame. I stared at him for a moment, and then with my jaw set, I replied, "It … wasn't … my … call!"

Pap shot back, "You could have done something!"

And for the only time I can remember, I shouted at my dad in anger, turned my back to him, and stormed out. Normally, that kind of behavior was not tolerated, but this was anything but a normal situation.

As I flew into my bedroom, I threw myself on my bed. Through my tears, I stared at the bed across the room. It had been Chuck's. Chuck had come to work on our farm for that summer so we had shared the bedroom. It had been a great summer working side by side, getting to know each other, truly becoming best friends. We bragged about our football teams, goofed around, shared our hopes and dreams, and talked late into the night about our girlfriends. I was dating Molly Brotherton, the girl I planned to marry, and Chuck was in love with Yvonne Sturgill, a girl he had met at TTLC. He felt that the Lord was calling him into the ministry, and he was sure that Yvonne was going to be at his side as his bride.

Only now half the room was empty, and I wasn't going to take the blame. Through my burning tears, I kept saying to myself, "It wasn't my fault, it wasn't my fault!"

A few minutes passed and my mom quietly came into my room, sat on the edge of my bed, and began to rub my back, "Duane, I'm so sorry. No one is blaming you for what happened, especially Pap. All of us are reeling from what has happened, and he's just trying to understand. He just let his emotions come out in the wrong way."

I knew she was right. This was out of character for Pap. So I rolled onto my side and looked up at her and replied, "I know. It's okay."

With that, she leaned over and gave me a kiss, "We are so glad that you and Vernon are okay. We can't begin to imagine how much Aunt Mim and Uncle Bill are hurting right now."

When my mom left my room, she quietly closed the door behind her, unaware of the desperate struggle that was beginning in my heart. An ocean of thoughts began to flood over me, but I didn't want to deal with any of them.

Why did they drown and I didn't?

Could I have said or done something that would have prevented the tragedy?

We had a lifejacket in our canoe. Why hadn't I thought for Tim to put it on when I saw how bad the waves were? I knew he wasn't a good swimmer.

Why had I panicked and climbed into the swamped canoe?

Wave after wave of all the "would-have-should-haves" and "why-didn't-I-or-why-did-I's" relentlessly washed over me, threatening to drown me in a huge lake of guilt.

In the shock of all that had happened, the idea of blame hadn't even crossed my mind before now. Everything had happened so fast on Opeongo Lake that all I could concentrate on was the need of that moment. Now I was home, and the enormity of what had happened began to sink in.

Throughout the entire rescue process and ride home, I hadn't shed a tear. Though the tears had been building up and threatening to break through the dam I had erected, I'd been able to keep them in check—until my dad confronted me.

Now as I lay on my bed, the floodwaters of grief overwhelmed the dam and burst through all the barriers I had erected. My pillow became soaked with tears. Again and again, I yelled into my pillow, "It was not my fault! It was not my fault!" in hopes of convincing myself. My muffled plea did little to keep a deep, dark reality from rising to the surface.

It *was* my fault!

Three people were dead, and it was *my fault*!

When Don's canoe had swamped, and we had all maneuvered out of the submerged canoe, I had been the one who panicked. I had been the one who climbed into the swamped canoe and stood up. I had been the one who had set off the chain of events leading to their deaths. I couldn't escape that reality.

If I had kept my cool and not panicked, then we would have all been able to hang on to the swamped canoe and stay afloat until Bob's canoe returned from shore to rescue us. Faced with a life-or-death situation, I had failed miserably.

I thought I could handle pressure. In sports, I always enjoyed the games where the winner wasn't determined until the final buzzer and the lead changed hands almost every time down the court or the field. Those had been the games I wanted to play in because I believed I was the player who could be counted on in high-pressure situations to do his best. I fancied myself as a sports hero.

The reality was that this hero was actually a coward and a failure. Because of me, three friends were dead.

As all the emotions of guilt and failure washed over me, my pride wouldn't let me accept them. My tearful plea, "It was not my fault!" became a mantra that I kept repeating over and over again, helping me to erect a strong wall of denial encasing the truth.

A few minutes later, as I stood up from my bed to head downstairs, something caught my eye. The framed "Man of the Star" certificate hanging on the wall over my bed seemed to glare at me. Though just a few days before it was a proud reminder of personal accomplishment, it now mocked me. Even though the words said, "Honesty no matter the cost," "Always helpful to others," and "Outstanding leadership," I heard them shouting "Liar," "Phony," and "Loser."

"Shut up!" I said to the certificate as I turned and walked out of my room.

I walked downstairs and across the kitchen to the refrigerator. As I opened the door to grab a snack, my dad came in and with tears in his eyes, said, "Duane, I'm really sorry for what I said. I know it wasn't your fault. Will you forgive me?"

"Yeah. I understand," was my short reply as I stuck out my hand to him and we shook hands. I looked him in the eyes and said, "It's okay."

After finishing my snack, I climbed into my car and headed over to my girlfriend's house. Molly met me at the door and broke into tears, "Oh, Duane, I'm so sorry," she whispered as we stood there and embraced. "I'm so glad you are okay, but Chuck ..." Molly sobbed as her voice trailed off.

We walked silently to the rec room in the basement and sat, facing each other, on the couch by the pool table. Molly quietly listened with tears streaming down her face as I described in detail everything that had happened.

By the time I had finished, Molly's dad had come home from work. Normally, there would have been a lot of hustle and bustle in the house, but that evening, there was a heavy silence. We went upstairs and found Molly's parents, grandmother, and Molly's older brother and sister watching TV in the den. As we walked into the room, Molly's dad turned the TV off.

Since Chuck and I had become more or less joined at the hip that summer, almost every time I went to Molly's house, Chuck came with me. Many evenings were spent with him swimming or playing pool or watching TV with Molly's family when I was hanging out there. As a result, he had become close to them.

Molly and I sat on the organ bench in the den as I recounted again all that had happened in the accident and our rescue. Only this time, when I started to describe my actions when Don's canoe swamped, I choked on the words, "...and I climbed into the swamped canoe." I didn't want to look like a failure in front of Molly's family, so I changed the story a little.

"Someone climbed into the canoe."

Molly shot a glance at me, not knowing what to think, but she never said anything.

When I finished, they had a lot of the same questions that I was slowly growing accustomed to answering. As we talked, we began to reminisce about Chuck.

"He was always so much fun to have around. That husky laugh of his was so contagious."

"He is the last person I would have ever thought would drown. He was such a good swimmer. It seemed that he was always racing someone in swimming."

"He was always so friendly. I remember the first time he came over, I felt like I had known him for a long time."

The conversation went on for a while until it was time for me to head home.

As I made the thirty-minute drive home that night, my car must have been on autopilot, since I know I wasn't paying any attention to the road. I was totally lost in thought. The images of my telling the story of the accident kept playing in my mind as I wrestled with my conscience. *What I said is the truth. Why do other people need to know that I was the one? I feel bad enough as it is, why do I have to carry this burden. Isn't it enough to tell what happened without saying who did it?*

Little did I know how my deflecting the truth was putting me on the dangerous slippery slope of denial. All I knew was that it seemed to slightly ease my pain.

That night I was able to marshal my defenses around me. I developed a train of thought that would turn away any accusations of guilt and keep me from facing the reality of my actions: Since "God causes all things to work for good," who am I to say that what happened was bad? After all, three canoes had swamped and one person from each canoe had drowned. Clearly, it must have been God's will that they were dead and somehow God was going to use this for good. I was simply a player in God's grand scheme of things, so who was I to question Him? Those three guys would have died whether or not

I had even been on the trip. Therefore, I had no reason to feel guilty, and I could mourn their deaths with hope.

Armed with this twisted rationale, I was ready to move on. I talked openly and freely about the accident, telling anyone who would listen. I always praised God for his miraculous intervention and quoted Romans 8:28, but I was always careful not to mention my actions of climbing into the swamped canoe. Whenever I came to that part of the story, I would simply repeat what I had said to Molly's family, "Someone climbed into the swamped canoe and stood up, forcing it down and out of reach—setting off a chain of events that led to the deaths."

I would always be very careful to tell the truth about what had happened on Opeongo Lake that day; I just wouldn't tell the whole truth. I used the truth to mislead people.

The next week or so was a blur of calling hours, funerals, and travel. Vernon and I were able to make it to Tim's visitation hours, but we couldn't attend his funeral because our family left the next morning for Chicago to attend Chuck's funeral.

My cousin's funeral was held at his church, Village Bible Church. When my family arrived, the church was already filling up. We found our way to the seats roped off for the family in the front pews. Soon the church sanctuary was packed with many people standing in the back and along the sides. As soon as I sat down, the reality of his death and the role I had played in it kept being hammered home. It was an open-casket service, and I couldn't take my eyes off Chuck's lifeless body. The casket was below the pulpit. I tried to stop looking at him and look instead at the speaker, but every time I did my eyes were immediately diverted back to the casket. As I sat there, a fly landed on his upper lip and crawled into his nose—accentuating the reality of his death. I sat there in shock, staring at his body whispering, "I'm so sorry, Chuck," over and over. But even in the midst of all of this, I was able to keep my emotions under control and my tears in check.

As soon as the service was over I wanted to escape, but I had no way to leave or place to go. I felt trapped. Again and again people came up to me after the service and asked, "Duane, what happened?" Depending on who was asking and how much time I had to answer, I would give either a condensed version of the story or the full account. I told the story so many times that I felt like I was a robot just repeating what I had been programed to say. I was always careful never to say that I was the one who climbed into the canoe. But each time I told it, I found myself believing more of my own deception. Soon the truth of my actions was safely locked in the deep recesses of my memory.

On the second Saturday after the accident, a memorial service was held at Trail to Life Camp for all three of the guys. At first the service was to be held in the camp lodge, but it was full to overflowing more than an hour before the service was to begin, so it as moved outside. Around one thousand people filled the hill between the lodge and the headquarters building. Sitting under the stars seemed the right place to be as we lifted our voices in praise singing many favorite camp songs, and as we heard testimony after testimony about Don, Chuck, and Tim. A pastor who was a good friend of Don's gave an evangelistic message built on the testimony of the three guys. When the altar call was given, scores of people responded, expressing faith in Christ.

I did share briefly during the testimony time about the impact Don and Chuck had on my life, but not about the accident. I didn't want to talk about what had happened. I was ashamed of what I had done and was scared of talking about it. I was with the people who knew the full truth, and they would be able to see and expose my ruse.

Little did I realize how I had allowed myself to be deceived. The irony in it all was that I used Scripture to stray away. Romans 8:28 is a beautiful verse that is full of hope, but I took it out of context and used it as an excuse to hide from personal responsibility. My pride wouldn't allow me to feel guilty.

This form of temptation is the same one Satan used when he tempted Jesus in the wilderness. The gospels of Matthew, Mark, and Luke all record how Satan took Jesus to the pinnacle of the temple and told Him to jump in order to prove that He was the Son of God. Satan even quoted Psalms 91:11–12 out of context as part of the temptation, but Jesus exposed the deceptive way Satan was using Scripture. Jesus then properly used the Word of God to stand strong against the wiles of the Devil to defeat the temptation.

I had read these passages in Scripture but failed to see how they related to me. As a result, I took the bait hook, line, and sinker, never realizing how easy it is to rationalize sin by taking Bible verses out of context.

I had successfully blocked the truth off in my mind, but each time I told the story, something happened in my heart. It was as if each accounting placed a small pebble in my heart. At first I didn't notice, but as weeks turned into months and then into years, I began to be weighed down by depression as the weight of those pebbles increased.

I don't think anyone was aware of my burden of guilt as time went on. Even though many good things had happened to me—Molly and I were married, I graduated from college, I directed Trail to Life Camp for a year, we moved to Denver, Colorado, to attend seminary, and our first daughter was born—I couldn't shake the guilt. I felt as if I was a total failure. The fear of someday facing another life-or-death situation consumed me. It wasn't that I was afraid of dying—I had been to death's door when I was sinking into the depths of Opeongo Lake, and I knew it wasn't terrifying. What shook me to the core was the thought of ever being in a situation where I might be responsible if someone got hurt.

The depression didn't come on me all at once. It started with a chilling sensation that I would get whenever I would tell someone about the accident. I would get very cold regardless of how warm it was around me. After a while, I would begin to shake, and my voice would quiver whenever I told my account of the accident. I was having flashbacks, and I would feel as cold as I did when I first came out of Opeongo Lake and crawled into the tent.

I can still recall how this troubling feeling began for me—and it started not long after the accident.

Immediately after the memorial service at TTLC, summer two-a-day football practices started, giving me a welcome diversion from the distress of the previous two weeks. I had numerous opportunities to share about the accident with teammates and witness to them, but I always used my safe version of the account—which only added more pebbles of guilt to my heart. What is interesting, though, is that nobody ever asked me who climbed into the boat and stood up. If they had, I probably would have lied to cover up my deception.

Already, my façade of acceptance and healing was beginning to deteriorate, slowly transporting me to the shores of a limitless lake of depression and throwing me into its deepest part. At first, I was able to tread water and even make progress toward shore. For instance, talking with Uncle Bill and Pastor Gaskell, and attending the funerals and memorial services helped to start bringing closure—drawing me closer to the shore of healing.

I actually began to think I could make it to solid ground and keep my secret safe, but with each altered retelling of the events, the number of the pebbles of guilt accumulating in my heart increased, and their weight began to pull me down.

Making it to shore no longer seemed possible. Simply surviving became my priority. I was drowning in guilt, but instead of a heavy hiking boot and wet clothes pulling me down, the weight of the accumulating tiny pebbles of guilt kept me under the surface.

Any sense of accomplishment I might experience would be swept away, slowly draining my desire and will to make it to the surface. It wasn't water in my lungs that caused the excruciating pain but despair in my heart. Because I had chosen deception, I once again found myself on the bottom of a lake drowning—but now in an overwhelming storm of failure and guilt. I was hopeless, and unless something changed or someone came to my rescue, eventually I was going down for good.

CHAPTER ELEVEN

SET FREE

Three men were dead, and it was my fault.

Nothing could change that. Not even a significant passage of time could alter the bitter reality that lived inside my soul.

No matter what I did, I couldn't escape the weight of the guilt. Self-condemnation became my constant companion. I felt that I was an untrustworthy failure, and steering clear of me was the safest and best thing anyone could do. Any confidence or ability to cope that I appeared to possess was a carefully guarded façade. All personal victories or successes came complete with a nagging sense of failure. Nothing lightened the load I carried.

They say time heals all wounds. I say that is not true. Indeed, after seven and a half years had passed since the accident, my battle continued. And by then my secret struggle was starting to show itself to others.

By this time, I was in my final year at Denver Seminary, and I was facing the stress of an intense oral examination in front of professors, putting my resume together, and finding a ministry position upon graduation.

The pressure was intense. It was a do-or-die situation: if I didn't pass orals, I wouldn't graduate. However, even if I did succeed with the exam, that was just the beginning of my pressures. Passing and graduation would mean I needed to find a church willing to hire a failure like me. I was sure of two things: I would fail orals or if I made it through orals, no church would hire someone who had a huge "F" burned onto his forehead.

I began to withdraw and pull inside. Sleep became my escape.

Molly and I had been married now for three years, and we had welcomed our first child, Katie, into our lives. It was a good thing I had them, for knowing that I had to provide for Molly and Katie was the only thing that kept me from allowing myself to sink into the depths of depression.

Morning after morning the alarm would ring. I would turn it off, roll over, and go back to sleep—not wanting to face another day. Then, at the last possible second, I would wake up and rush to class. Showering, shaving, and brushing my teeth became optional. I'm sure I wasn't a pleasure to sit next to in class, but I simply didn't care. Personal hygiene went out the window.

No doubt Molly saw what was happening, but neither of us spoke about it. The crazy schedule I kept with a full load of classes—studying and providing for my family—gave me something convenient to hide behind.

One day, just as my Creative Bible Teaching class was ending, the professor, Dr. Dennis Williams, turned to me and said: "Duane, could you stay after class for a few minutes?"

As the classroom emptied, I walked nervously to the front of the room and waited for him to finish answering a question of a classmate. After the room was empty, he turned to me and spoke. He said, "Duane, I'm really concerned about you. There is no doubt in my mind about your call to the ministry, and you are doing well academically. What worries me is you how poorly you do with public speaking. You are a mess when you get in front of people. If you don't get help right away, you won't last one year in the pastorate."

He continued, "My wife is a speech professor at the University of Denver, and I know she can help you. It just so happens that in

two weeks she is beginning an evening public speaking class here at
the seminary that is open to the community. I think you should take
advantage of it."

He was right. I needed help. So on a Thursday evening, two
weeks later, I found myself walking into her class.

The fact that I needed this remedial help was a shock to me. In
high school I had been in a number of activities that required public
performance and leadership. I played varsity football and basketball,
was president of the school band, and had a minor role in a school
drama. I had even run for senior class president—and lost.

What was also ironic was that at one time public speaking didn't
bother me. As a high school sophomore, I had won the public speaking contest for our chapter of Future Farmers of America, beating
our chapter's defending champion. I then represented our chapter at
the FFA state public speaking competition.

When I was graduating from Malone University, I was asked to
share my testimony at the baccalaureate service, speaking before an
auditorium full of classmates, family members, and friends.

But now, just a little over two years later, I cowered before a small
classroom of my seminary peers. My shame and fear of failing was
taking control of my life.

I didn't understand what was happening, but I knew something
had to change. The speech class helped deal with symptoms, but it
didn't touch the root cause. I knew I needed help, but I didn't know
where to turn. I was drowning, and the weight of all the pebbles of
denial in my heart was threatening to pull me under once and for all.

But one day it all changed.

I was enrolled in a pastoral counseling skills course at the seminary. Part of the class included a weekly, two-hour, hands-on session
where we practiced the skills and techniques of counseling with one
another. Typically, one person would counsel another classmate for
fifteen minutes while two other students and a facilitator observed.
Then, for the next fifteen minutes we would discuss the strengths

and weaknesses in the counseling techniques used. We would then rotate roles with a new counselor and counselee. The counselee was required to talk about real issues in his life.

Midway through the fall quarter, my group met, and I was first to play the role of counselee. At the time I was working part-time as a professional window washer, so I shared how I was toying with the idea of quitting the company I was working for, buying my own equipment, and starting my own window washing business.

During the conversation, the counselor made a crucial observation. He looked at me and said, "It sounds like the only thing that is holding you back is that you are afraid of failing. Has there ever been a time when you experienced a big failure?"

I sat in my chair speechless for a few moments, staring at him and debating with myself whether or not to share my failure. I wanted to keep up the charade and say "No," but I just couldn't do it. The weight of all the guilt over the past several years was overwhelming!

So I shook my head yes and proceeded to share the entire account of the canoeing accident. Our facilitator had the wisdom to allow me to continue to talk, and all four of my classmates helped me talk through my failure for the remaining hour and forty-five minutes.

As always, I was shivering with cold as I shared all the details, but this time, when I came to the part where I usually said, "Someone climbed into the swamped canoe and stood up," I was honest. For the first time since I sat in Molly's parents' house and misrepresented what had happened, I told the whole truth. I took full responsibility for my actions. I couldn't keep that secret anymore. I had to own up to it.

I continued, telling them of the deaths of Don, Chuck, and Tim, and I explained how I had almost been a fourth victim. I told of our rescue and of the miraculous occurrences surrounding it. I finished the account with my standard explanation of Romans 8:28 in my attempt to deflect any responsibility for the deaths: "God causes all things to work for good," I said. However, this time it just sounded hollow.

My counselor looked at me and said, "It really sounds like you feel guilty for climbing into that canoe and standing up. Do you?"

I wanted to shout, "YOU BET!" Instead, I looked at him and quietly whispered, "Yes."

He responded, "What does the Lord want you to do with your guilt?"

"Confess it," was my short reply, and then I went on to quote to them 1 John 1:8–9: "If we say we have no sin, we deceive ourselves, and the truth is not in us. If we confess our sins, he is faithful and just to forgive us our sins and to cleanse us from all unrighteousness."

"Do you want to do that?" he asked me.

"Yes," was my quiet, yet firm reply. With my elbows on my desk, I bowed my head against my folded hands and cried out, "O God ..."

The dam holding back my tears burst. I wept and I confessed to the Lord all the guilt and shame I had carried all those years. I poured out my heart to Christ and took full responsibility for all my actions and failures.

The guys pulled their desks in tight around me and placed their hands on my shoulders and knees and began praying along with me as I called out to the Lord and allowed the Holy Spirit to do His convicting and cleansing work in me. I held nothing back.

As I cried and confessed, I felt the overwhelming cleansing power of Jesus flood over and through my heart and soul. The tailgate of my heart was released, and all the pebbles of guilt and denial were dumped out in a huge pile at the foot of the cross of Jesus.

I was forgiven!

I was free!

I was experiencing the reality the Bible so clearly describes: "Wretched man that I am! Who will deliver me from this body of death? Thanks be to God through Jesus Christ our Lord! ... There

is therefore now no condemnation for those who are in Christ Jesus"
(Romans 7:24–25, 8:1).

In the days and years since that life-changing moment, I've come to
realize that for all that time I had been locked in a long battle with
my own pride.

Pride put me on the slippery slope of denial. I did not want to
accept responsibility for any of my actions that might have contributed to the deaths of my friends. Pride helped me twist the meaning of Romans 8:28 into a convenient escape hatch. Pride kept me
from accepting my feelings of guilt—even though I was drowning
in them.

My guilt was a selfish emotion. My sorrow was not over sins
committed but over my failure to live up to personal ideals. I was
more concerned with what others would think of me if they knew
how I had panicked than I was with telling the truth. My reputation
was more important to me than the harm I had caused others.

Pride caused me to live a lie. I tried and wanted to believe that
nothing was wrong, but in reality, I was denying Christ and rejecting
His ability to cleanse me.

I had set a standard for myself that was higher than the perfect
standard of God. If God is able to forgive me, but I am not able to
forgive myself, then my standard must be higher than God's—which
makes me my own god. No wonder I was sinking!

When I prayed that day and confessed my heart to the Lord, I
wasn't just confessing remorse over a moment of panic and weakness,
I was confessing a boatload of serious sins and sinful attitudes that I
had allowed to grow in my heart since that first incident. I faced my
guilt and admitted the source of the filth: the pride I had allowed to
take hold of my heart.

For all that time, I had refused to face the thought that I needed to confess my guilt to the Lord. Confession was a negative idea to me. It conjured up childhood memories of spankings that usually followed any admission of guilt. One thing I didn't want was pain added to my guilt. Therefore, I resisted the only thing that could bring real healing to my life.

My friends in that class helped me see that biblical confession has a totally different meaning from what I thought it was. Confession does not bring added pain! It opens the door to the compassion of Christ. It does not bring punishment! It allows forgiveness to take place. The apostle Paul put it this way: "For godly grief produces a repentance that leads to salvation without regret, whereas worldly grief produces death" (2 Corinthians 7:10).

This refreshing new understanding of forgiveness and salvation reminded me of that awful day in Opeongo Lake when I was fighting to stay alive. My friends Bob and Wes had paddled their canoe out to rescue me. They came to where I was, and they simply offered to help. With their arrival, they brought hope and salvation to me and the other guys in the water.

At the time I didn't realize it, but I had a decision to make: deny my need, deny their help, and drown—or realize my need, accept their help, and live. I didn't have to think about that decision at all.

As soon as Bob and Wes were close enough, I let go of the swamped canoe I had been clinging to and grabbed hold of their safe and steady canoe. (I hung on so tightly I may have even left finger marks in the side of their canoe!) The moment I felt the solid rock of shore under my feet, I let go of the canoe and put my full weight on the rock.

What a great picture of confession and forgiveness! My classmates found me floundering in The Lake of Guilt and Depression and brought me to shore by speaking God's truth into my life. However, I was the one who had to decide whether to accept their help and live, or deny it and continue on my path of self-destruction. Once I chose to confess my guilt to the Lord, He picked me up out of the mess I had made, cleansed me of my guilt and shame, and set my feet on the rock. The psalmist put it so clearly when he wrote: "He drew me up from the pit of destruction, out of the miry bog, and set my feet upon a rock, making my steps secure. He put a new song in my mouth, a song of praise to our God" (Psalm 40:2–3).

After I confessed my sins and experienced forgiveness, I soon discovered that the apostle Peter was becoming an example for me. He was a proud, fast-acting man and a leader among the apostles, but when the pressure was on and he faced a threatening situation, he too panicked and did exactly what he had pledged he would never do: He denied the Lord. Peter denied the man he loved and respected more than anyone else. He denied the person for whom he had pledged a willingness to die. When Jesus needed him the most, Peter turned his back and denied Him—not just once, but three times.

The instant the words of denial rolled off his lips the third time, he heard a rooster crow, reminding him of Jesus's warning that this would happen. Luke tells us that Jesus turned and looked straight at Peter (Luke 22:61). Jesus was being falsely accused, slapped, spit on, and punched; yet He turned and locked eyes with Peter for a moment. With that look, Peter instantly realized what he had done. He had failed Jesus, and as far as Peter was concerned, his actions were going to contribute to Jesus's death. He knew he was a total failure and was guilty of turning his back on the man he had come to know as the Messiah, the Savior of the world, God in the flesh, and his close friend.

I can only imagine the depth of guilt, shame, and remorse that washed over him and began to crush him under its weight.

Peter dealt with his guilt differently than I did mine. He went out and "wept bitterly" (Matthew 26:75). He immediately faced his failure and dealt with his grief and guilt. It is easy to imagine him running blindly down street after street, past house after house until he threw himself into the dark shadows of an alley and wailed in grief—his body convulsing with sorrow and guilt. He didn't run from his sorrow, he didn't stuff his guilt, he didn't allow his pride to take control; he faced his brokenness and experienced the full weight of what he had done.

But the story doesn't end there.

On the morning of Jesus's resurrection, an angel appeared to the women who had come to the tomb where Jesus was buried, and he spoke these words: "You seek Jesus of Nazareth, who was crucified. He has risen; he is not here. See the place where they laid him. But go, tell his disciples and Peter" (Mark 16:6–7).

"... and Peter."

It's as if the angel were saying: "Be sure Peter knows that Jesus is alive. Peter needs to know that he is forgiven. Peter needs to have his memory of his terrible failure healed."

The Lord reached down to Peter—who was drowning in guilt and remorse, and whose heart was shattered—with the only message that could lift Peter out of the pit of despair: "Peter, I'm alive and you are forgiven!"

Since the day I confessed my guilt over my actions during the canoe accident, I have not been able to read those words "... and Peter" without stopping and hearing the Lord saying to me, "... and Duane."

By carrying my guilt and shame for all that time, I had in essence been denying Jesus and His ability to forgive and cleanse me. I was carrying a burden that I was not capable of carrying nor was even supposed to be carrying. Though I had received total forgiveness of all my sins when I received Christ as my Savior, I foolishly chose to hang on to one sin, one failure.

Once I had responded to the Lord's patient, gracious call, the burden was gone. I was free!

CHAPTER TWELVE

DETAILS MATTER

"Just the facts, ma'am."

I don't know how many times I heard fictional Los Angeles police detective Joe Friday say those words on the TV show *Dragnet* as we huddled around our family's fifteen-inch black-and-white TV in our living room when I was growing up. But those black-and-white words of admonition were ground in me in my formative years. Accuracy of the facts was important because they led to understanding truth.

This principle was to rise up and smack me in the face within days of returning home after the accident on Opeongo Lake.

Those first days felt like one continuous blur. I was numb and emotionally drained. My spirit was adrift on a lake in the middle of a storm: It had no direction and no paddle. My spirit was at the mercy of the wind and waves. I found myself looking forward to church on Sunday because it was a safe harbor from the storm.

When Sunday arrived, I felt like I was crawling up the rocky shore again, exhausted and overwhelmed with pain. I was bruised and battered, and I ached for the encouragement of God's Word along with healing power of worship. I needed to be able to focus on the Lord and allow His presence to comfort and strengthen me.

As Molly and I slid into our usual pew at church with a few

friends from the youth group, I felt a presence of the Lord come over me. Just as we settled into the familiar padded pews, the choir began singing. The voices filled the cavernous church sanctuary with an opening song of praise. Their singing, as well as the Scripture reading and special music, seemed to wash over my soul. I sat with my eyes closed soaking in His presence—allowing myself to rest and be refreshed.

Just before our pastor, Ralph Neighbor Sr., led the congregation in the pastoral prayer, he said, "I'm afraid I have some sad news to share with you this morning about a terrible tragedy that occurred with Trail to Life Camp." Then he shared the news of the canoeing accident and the deaths of Don, Chuck, and Tim. I was jolted back to reality. Rest and refreshment were over.

My church, Church of the Open Door in Elyria, Ohio, had direct ties to Trail to Life Camp. Several people from the church had been part of the core group that helped start the camp. Every year children and teens from the church attended the camp. As Pastor Neighbor shared about the accident, gasps and sobs echoed throughout the congregation. The shock of the tragedy had hit home.

For me, however, the shock was not from hearing the announcement of the deaths of my friends but from the fact that my pastor's account of the accident was wrong. He was telling an entirely different story:

"Apparently, they were camped on an island when strong winds caused a canoe with three teenage boys in it to capsize. Don Enzor, the director of Trail to Life Camp, saw their plight and paddled out to help them. In the confusion of the rescue attempt, his canoe also capsized. One of the teens panicked and grabbed Don, pulling them both under. Before it was all over, Don and two teenage boys drowned."

Pastor Neighbor continued, "One of the boys who drowned was Chuck Schnittker. Though Chuck was from Chicago, he has been working in the area on his uncle's farm this summer. Many of you know his uncle and aunt, Dwight and Shirley Miller of Miller Orchards. Chuck has been an active member of our youth ministry these past two months."

As I heard his rendition of the account, I fought the urge to stand up and shout, "That's not what happened!" Instead, I shook my head and quietly said to myself, "He just doesn't have the facts."

The church service continued, but all I could think of was the accident. My eyes had been taken off the Lord and focused again on my heartache.

When the service was over, I was numb. As I walked blindly through the lobby, I heard the voices of people expressing their condolences, and I felt them shake my hand—but it was as if I were in a dream. I passed several of the guys who had been on the trip, but we really didn't say anything to each other. We only knowingly shook our heads and shrugged our shoulders. Al DesChamps was the only person from the trip I spoke to, and that was simply to say, "I wonder where he got his information." Interestingly, I think that was the only time I ever said anything to him about the canoe accident.

The next day I gained insight into a possible source of our pastor's erroneous account. I received a letter from a relative. Inside was a newspaper article about the accident. Apparently, news of the accident had hit the wire services, and the story had been printed in a number of newspapers in Ohio. One of the wire services had printed wrong information about the accident, and it was the same story Pastor Neighbor had shared. Over the next several weeks, I continued to receive a number of newspaper clippings from a variety of cities. Some were spot on, while others left me wondering about the source of their information. Someone had given a reporter the wrong details about what had occurred, and it was being repeated as fact.

I began to wrestle with how to combat this misinformation. I'm sure the intensity of my feelings was ramped up by the internal struggle I was having and the guilt I was carrying. Conflicting thoughts flooded my mind: "What difference did it really make? Nothing would change what had happened. Three young men were still dead. So what if the details were being misrepresented? Isn't truth what you make it? What may be true for you might not be true for me. We simply need to be sincere in our belief, right?"

I couldn't shake the reality that details *do* matter. They are the facts that form the foundation for what is true—and truth is always important. This desire to protect the facts motivated me to do something totally out of character.

One evening right after the start of school, I was in my bedroom and was thinking about what Pastor Neighbor had said. Before I knew it, I was sitting at my desk writing my account of what had happened.

As I wrote, I felt a heavy burden lift from my heart. I had a written form of the memory that flooded my mind, so I no longer needed to carry the weight of trying to remember all the details though I did intentionally leave out the details of my actions when Don's canoe swamped. Writing also forced me to better organize my thoughts and work through my memories of everything that had happened, making sure they were accurate.

When I finished writing, I didn't know what to do with the manuscript, so I decided to take it to school.

A couple of weeks later, Mrs. White, my English teacher, was surprised when I handed her my account of the accident and asked her for feedback. I had never written anything that wasn't an assignment or extra credit. I was a decent student who enjoyed school, but I had never let school get in the way of my education. Schoolwork usually came after fun, sports, and friends. Mrs. White was happy to read it.

The next day, as I walked into class, she asked me to come up to her desk. As she handed me the paper, she quietly said, "Duane, it means a lot to me that you would share something so dramatic and personal with me. I am so sorry and my heart breaks for you. Please understand that if you feel you need to talk more about it, I am here."

I thanked her, and turned and walked to my desk.

This written account has served as a vital source of information for me through the years. It became one of my most treasured items. When Molly and I were married in 1974, I took it with me as we moved into our first apartment, and it has gone with us to every subsequent apartment or house since then. As a youth pastor, and later as a senior pastor, I would sometimes read it before sharing my testimony with a large group, or before leading a teenage or young adult wilderness canoe trip. It has anchored me to the facts and truth as I retold the story again and again.

As time passed, I felt the impact of the misinformed accounts less keenly. However, in 2008 I was in Algonquin Provincial Park with a group of young adults. We had just finished a wilderness canoe trip and stopped by the park's visitor center before heading home. At the gift shop I picked up S. Bernard Shaw's book, *Lake Opeongo: Untold Stories of Algonquin Park's Largest Lake*. While leafing through the book, I came across a short account of the canoe accident. There it was. A similar account to what pastor gave that day in church plus some additional misinformation.

There were several discrepancies in Shaw's account relating to who our group was, plus the date of the accident was off by one day. It was upsetting to read, "Notorious shifting winds off Windy Point capsized several canoes.... One of the leaders, a powerful swimmer, righted the canoes and hoisted the boys inside but one panicked, grabbed him, and they both disappeared. A second boy also drowned in the confusion."[*]

I stood in the store staring in disbelief at what I had read. His source of information was based on the wrong accounts that had been circulated soon after the accident. Even the location of the tragedy was wrong. The accident had occurred in the North Arm of Opeongo Lake, which is several miles from Windy Point.

---

[*]S. Bernard Shaw, *Lake Opeongo: Untold Stories of Algonquin Park's Largest Lake* (Renfrew, ON: General Store Publishing House, 1998), 40.

What disturbed me most was the hidden message conveyed in this account. I knew that Don Enzor was not the victim of his heroic attempt to rescue some panicking kids.

There were three true heroes that day. Three canoes swamped in the storm, and one person from each canoe drowned. Each willingly put his life on the line to try to help someone in need. They sacrificed their lives so their friends could live. No one held a gun to Don's head forcing him to turn around to help us pull Chuck, Dan, and Vernon from the water. Tim gave no thought to his own peril when he reached over the side of our canoe to help Vernon climb in. As things spiraled out of control and my canoe swamped, Don and Chuck came back to help when they could have continued toward the island and their own safety. They never intended to, but those three young men became heroes that day.

When I think of them, I am reminded of the words of Jesus: "Greater love has no one than this, that someone lay down his life for his friends" (John 15:13). Every guy involved in the accident and rescue literally lived out this verse by putting his life on the line for a friend that day. There were no self-centered actions. Our friends were in danger, and we needed to help. That is what true friends do. And friends putting their lives on the line to rescue friends is a truth worth preserving.

Without accurate details and facts, the truth of that day would be lost, distorted, or forgotten—adding to an already tragic event. With the presence of accurate details, the truth lives on.

This is why my coming clean about my role in the tragedy was so very important.

Through the years I have had many conversations with a number of guys who were in the water that day, as well as with Chuck's parents. Again and again I would hear them say things like:

"I remember turning around and seeing Vernon caught under the canoe."

"When I grabbed the side of Don's canoe, Don yelled out not to pull down on it, but to swim with every ounce of our strength."

"I felt so helpless when Don's canoe swamped. There wasn't anyone left to help us."

It shouldn't surprise anyone that the accounts of the eyewitnesses match up with each other. We were there. We heard the cries for help from those in the water. We felt the icy cold water when our canoes overturned. We were in the middle of it all, and memories of something as traumatic as that don't disappear.

That is the beauty of truth—it is not something that is just thought up. It can be verified. The level of sincerity of belief doesn't determine whether or not something is true. Truth is based on facts and details. Objective, absolute truth does exist, and the facts and details back it up.

CHAPTER THIRTEEN

THE BIG PICTURE

What if that bear had not raided the food supply of the family camped on the North Arm of Opeongo Lake, causing the chain of events that led to our being rescued? What if that family had chosen a different campsite? What if they had decided on a different vacation altogether? What if we had decided to circumvent the perimeter of the North Arm instead of canoeing across it, parallel to the wind and waves? What if all the canoes had turned around and come back to help in the rescue? What if ... what if ... what if ...?

A thousand "what if" questions flooded my mind in the weeks and months following the canoeing accident. Each had imaginary answers, but none could change anything—and that only added to my thickening fog of confusion over understanding what really had transpired.

The fog began to lift as I took a step back and started to look at what had happened.

As I began to wrestle through the memories of that day, I found myself moving from my Sunday school level of understanding of God and His Word to a deeper and more intimate grasp of who God is and how He works in His creation. Many people learn great truths through study and research, but for me I learn more by doing and experiencing truth. I didn't realize it, but as I was sinking into the depths of Opeongo Lake, the Lord was enrolling me in an advanced school of theology.

The events surrounding the canoeing accident provided a framework for insight while the Scriptures gave me the truth I needed to begin putting the pieces together. Both served as a guide as I worked my way through my various biblical and theological classes and the research I had to do as part of my college and seminary education. As I wrestled with the intricacies and ramifications of competing doctrines and schools of thought within evangelical Christianity, I found myself continually returning to the same evaluation grid: What does the Bible say on the subject, and is this how I saw it demonstrated in the events surrounding the canoeing accident? When my situation or experience did not line up with what I was reading in the Bible, I realized that either I was misinterpreting my experience or I had a misunderstanding of what the Bible taught and needed to dig deeper. I could not interpret the Bible in light of my experiences, but rather needed to interpret my experiences in light of the Bible.

The canoeing accident helped develop my understanding of how the sovereignty of God and the freewill of humanity work together in prayer. The sovereignty of God speaks to the fact that God is the almighty, all-powerful Lord God, and He rules and reigns from His throne in heaven, accomplishing His will throughout creation. God is ultimately in control.

The prophet Isaiah put it like this: "It is he who sits above the circle of the earth, and its inhabitants are like grasshoppers; who stretches out the heavens like a curtain, and spreads them like a tent to dwell in" (Isaiah 40:22).

The psalmist wrote: "But you, O Lord, are enthroned forever; and you are remembered throughout all generations" (Psalm 102:12).

And Paul, writing to the church at Ephesus, said, "In him we have obtained an inheritance, having been predestined according to the purpose of him who works all things according to the counsel of his will, so that we who were the first to hope in Christ might be to the praise of his glory" (Ephesians 1:11–12).

The freewill of humanity describes the power God has given us to choose between right or wrong, good or evil, righteousness or sin. It is the greatest power given to us by God. Regardless of our circumstances or how relentlessly trials and temptations might hammer on us, we always have the power to choose our response. "Choose this day whom you will serve, ... But as for me and my house, we will serve the LORD" (Joshua 24:15).

The tension between these two teachings has created much confusion and misunderstanding through the years, but both the freewill of humanity and the sovereignty of God are clearly taught in the Bible. Since ordinary people wrote the Bible with a message for ordinary people, it shouldn't cause confusion. The very nature of Scripture is so simple that a child can grasp its meaning, while the greatest minds cannot begin to fathom the depths of its teachings.

As I personally worked through these doctrines, I continually flashed back to the canoeing accident. For example, when did God start to answer our prayer? When I first heard the cries for help from Chuck, Vernon, and Dan, and I turned and saw them struggling to get out of their canoe, I remember praying out loud, "Lord, help them."

With each stroke of my paddle as we turned into the waves and wind and started back to help them, I prayed for help and guidance to know what to do to rescue them. We were heading into uncharted water. None of us had any experience rescuing someone while in a canoe in the midst of strong winds and big waves, and we were scared. I'm confident I was not the only one praying at that moment.

Did God begin to answer our prayers and start to help us the moment we prayed, or was he already intervening on our behalf? There is no doubt in my mind that God was already involved. The question is, "When did He start?"

I have always believed that God hears and answers my prayers, but I used to visualize that when I prayed, God would hear my prayer and then respond. He would be sitting on His throne ruling the universe when a special phone would ring. I was calling to share my prayer request with Him, He would chat with me for a few minutes to get an understanding of what I needed, and then He would hang up. Turning to one of the angels He would say, "Looks like Duane has messed things up again and dug himself into a hole. Let's see what we can do to help him out …"

However, nothing could be further from the truth. The truth is that God, being infinite in His knowledge and wisdom, began at creation all the processes needed to have the answer to every prayer ever made in place at precisely the right moment. The writer of Hebrews puts it this way: "His works were finished from the foundation of the world. For he has somewhere spoken of the seventh day in this way: 'And God rested on the seventh day from all his works'" (Hebrews 4:3–4).

What a beautiful picture of the sovereignty of God at work! God knew in eternity past just what was needed on that day when we cried out, "Help, Lord!" and He had already answered our prayer. God rested on the seventh day with everything in place He needed to accomplish His will. That is why we are invited to enter into His rest in Hebrews 3:7–4:13.

To understand God's sovereignty, step back and think about just one aspect of the rescue. What was needed in order for that one boat to be on Opeongo Lake the morning of the accident? How was it that it happened to go past the island where many of the campers were stranded?

A hungry bear needed to raid a specific family's campsite. Before it could do that, the bear had to learn that campsites often provided plenty of good, easy food. Before it could learn that, the bear needed to be born and taught how to forage for food. Before this could happen, the bear's parents needed to be born and the parents of those bears and so on and so on; all the way back to Noah, when the bear's ancestors climbed on board an ark. Those bears' ancestors lived in the garden of Eden.

At any time something could have happened to interrupt the process: a plague that would have wiped out the bear population in that part of Canada, or a hunter could have killed one of the ancestors before it could have the necessary offspring. There are an infinite number of details that had to occur throughout the ages in order for a simple, hungry black bear to be in exactly the right place at the right time to start the chain of events that led to our rescue. This was not a coincidence. The Lord answered one of our prayers before we even uttered a word of it.

Because God is truly sovereign, no problem, no issue, and no circumstance is too big or too small for Him. He is aware of and is addressing them all in his perfect timing. I find this so encouraging and full of hope.

But if God is sovereign, were we just puppets on a string, doing His bidding when we went on the canoe trip? Where does our freewill fit into all of this?

Our freewill was just as much a part of what happened as the sovereignty of God. We chose not to have enough life jackets for everyone on the trip. We chose to end the trip early. We chose to wear our hiking boots and work shoes in the canoes that day. We chose to head out into the storm. We chose to paddle parallel to the waves. The guys on the island chose to try to flag down the passing boat.

No one forced us to do any of those things. Sure, the leaders made some of the choices while others were group decisions or individual choices. But the fact remains that we were free to decide, and with each choice came consequences—some good, while others we came to regret. Good, bad, or indifferent, each choice we made contributed to what happened that horrific day.

The sovereignty of God and our freewill were intricately interwoven into each stitch of time. Each played a vital role in every aspect of every part of that day without overriding or negating the other one: They were interdependent. Like the "heads" and "tails" on a coin, both are equally a part of the coin, appearing to be opposites but inseparably connected.

This is how I see the sovereignty of God and the freewill of humanity working together. Each is distinct and has a clear role in the grand scheme of things we call life. Yet the Lord has established that they function inseparably together.

We struggle with rectifying the sovereignty of God with the freewill of humanity because our understanding of God is too small. Reading through the Bible allows us to discover that God is truly omnipotent. He is all-powerful, all-knowing, all-wise. He is love, light, and life as well as all truth, all justice, grace, and mercy. He is eternal and infinite in all His characteristics, attributes and powers, not only in the extent of each but in the number of them that He possesses.*

What this means is that God is so big and powerful, and so truly awesome, that He is able to give us freewill and use our decisions to accomplish His perfect will at precisely the instant He predestined in eternity past. How does He do that?

I have no idea. But then He is eternal, infinite God, and I am not.

In Romans 8:26–39, the apostle Paul paints a beautiful picture of the sovereignty of God and how it plays out in our everyday lives. It is a passage of hope, love, power, and victory for us as believers. Interwoven in the descriptions of the will of God, the call of God on our lives, and the predestination of God are some references to the level of intimacy and activity of God in our lives. These verses opened my eyes to a deeper level of understanding of prayer.

> Likewise the Spirit helps us in our weakness. For we do not know what to pray for as we ought, but the Spirit himself intercedes for us with groanings too deep for words.

---

*Ephesians 3:20; Psalm 139:5; Psalm 33:6, 7, 9; Psalm 139:1–4; Romans 16:27; 1 John 4:8; John 1:4–5; John 1:4; John 1:14; Psalm 111:7; Exodus 34:6; Deuteronomy 33:27; Psalm 90:2.

And he who searches hearts knows what is the mind of the Spirit, because the Spirit intercedes for the saints according to the will of God. Who is to condemn? Christ Jesus is the one who died—more than that, who was raised—who is at the right hand of God, who indeed is interceding for us. (Romans 8:26–27, 34)

Think about it. God the Holy Spirit knows the real, foundational cries of our hearts, and He is in an ongoing conversation with God the Father, carrying our hearts' cries to Him. At the same time, God the Son, Jesus, is also in a conversation with the Father about us, interceding for us.

When I put these truths together, I realize that the Trinity—Father, Son, Holy Spirit—is in an ongoing conversation about me and every other believer. When I go to Him in prayer, I am accepting an invitation to enter into a conversation that they were already having on my behalf!

When I cried out for help on Opeongo Lake that day, the Lord responded: "Don't worry, we know exactly what is going on and we have it handled already. But we want you to see that, 'we know that for those who love God all things work together for good, for those who are called according to his purpose'" (Romans 8:28).

What a source of encouragement! This reality, as well as my understanding of the sovereignty of God and our freewill, helped me work through the ramifications of what happened that day. It has expanded my understanding of the Lord, deepened my faith, and provided me with an anchor to hang onto whenever the storms of life rage. It became the foundation for my belief that things never go wrong, they only go different.

CHAPTER FOURTEEN

THE STORY CONTINUES

It was probably an hour or so after the accident that Bob and Wes returned from their trip out to the island on Opeongo Lake. The dry clothes and extra food that they brought back were a great relief.

We climbed out of the tent, some of us still wearing only our underwear, and stood shivering in the wind while we dug through the pile of dry clothes trying to find something that fit. As soon as we were dressed, we climbed back into the tent to get warm.

All the while, Jerry kept the fire blazing and continued to cook. As each can of corn, beans, beef stew, or Spam was warmed up, he brought it to the tent where we devoured it.

But soon I began to feel antsy. I needed to get out of the tent and get alone with my thoughts. The shock of what had happened and the immensity of it all were beginning to overwhelm me. I needed time and space to begin processing things, so I crawled out of the tent and made my way down to the large rock where we had all climbed out of the water after the accident.

This was not just a bad dream: It was reality. Three young men whom I loved and respected were dead, and I was alive. Why had I been able to crawl out of the water?

Why had I survived?

What was the reason all this was happening?

As I sat at the edge of the water staring out over the area where their bodies lay in their watery grave, I kept asking the Lord why I was miraculously saved and they weren't. He could have pulled them from the water just as He did me, but He hadn't. Why?

As I sat on that rock, I sensed the Lord opening my eyes to the eternal perspective of this event. Although he didn't answer the "why" question, he began to impress on me that I had been saved from drowning for a purpose: He wasn't done with me yet.

Even though Don, Chuck, and Tim were now with the Lord, the impact of their lives would continue on. They had finished the preseason and were now enjoying the game. Those of us who were left behind were being called up to take their place. We were being given the responsibility to carry on the work of building the kingdom of God on earth.

Suddenly I found myself in the midst of a spiritual crisis. I began to wrestle with who would be in charge of my life. Would I continue running my life myself, or was I willing to surrender my life totally to Jesus and live for Him? I somehow knew that the ramifications of this decision would shape the rest of my life.

As I sat on the edge of that lake, I had no idea what that meant for me or what the discipleship path of surrender to Jesus would look like. All I knew for sure was that I didn't want to waste this opportunity. I wanted what Jesus wanted of me. I spoke the desire of my heart that seemed to just well up inside me. There was no heavenly music—just the sound of the wind and waves hitting the shore. There were no tears or feelings of strong emotions. I simply had a heart-to-heart talk with the Lord like I had never had before. As we talked, a calm, peaceful sense enveloped me. The Lord was talking with me and telling me to follow Him regardless of the cost.

I stood up, and with a gust of cool wind blowing in my face, I looked out over the water where the three young men lay and spoke these words: "Lord, I don't know what it is that you want from me, but I'm willing to do it. I want to carry on what those guys started.

You rescued me from these waters for a purpose, and I am willing to make that the focus of my life."

That morning, I had awakened as an immature teenage boy, but now I stood on the shore of Opeongo Lake as a young man with a purpose. And it all happened simply because I said yes to serving the Lord.

I now had a life-focus. I was surprised at the impact it would have on me. Gone was the desire to play college football, and in its place was a growing desire to minister to people. That day was the beginning of my call into the pastorate.

I wish I could say that I was instantly taken from that shoreline decision and immediately fast-forwarded into a dynamic ministry. And I wish I didn't have to deal with the quagmire of guilt and shame that I went through. But neither was the case.

Instead, the Lord placed me on a path of discipleship that has included a number of different forms of headwinds, sore muscles, relentless rain, and sleepless nights—just like we experienced on this trip. Through it all, though, I always sensed the presence of the Lord, leading me, guiding me, calling me back to the path whenever I would stray from it—reminding me that I was a survivor for a reason. And as the years passed and I witnessed the extent of the impact of the lives and testimonies of Don, Chuck, and Tim, the Lord began to open my eyes to the mantle of ministry I carried.

All three of these young men loved the Lord wholeheartedly and wanted nothing more than to help other people meet Jesus personally and enter into a relationship with Him. Each one had a special and unique ministry of telling other people about Jesus.

Don's ministry as a non-denominational evangelist was expanding as his dynamic and effective preaching and teaching was becoming well known. It didn't matter if he was talking with a teenager one on one, speaking to a full church, or teaching the Bible at TTLC, his love for Jesus and the Word of God was contagious. He lived a life of surrender to the Lord, and he wanted nothing more than to hear the Lord say, when he met Him face to face, "Well done, good and faithful servant." You couldn't help but want to have the same relationship with Jesus that he had.

I had witnessed my cousin Chuck share the love of Jesus with friends as well as with total strangers with great sensitivity and compassion, and he did it with ease. He could bring Jesus into a conversation in such a natural and comfortable way that you would think he was talking about the weather or his favorite football team. He always seemed to have a gospel tract on him to give to the person he was talking with—and it always seemed to relate to their conversation.

When I was in Chicago to attend Chuck's funeral, a classmate of his came up to me as I was standing in the lobby of the church after the funeral and asked, "I understand that you are Chuck's cousin and that you were there when he drowned. Is that right?"

"Yes," I replied.

He continued, "I need to tell someone about what Chuck did for me. One day, I was really down. Everything was going wrong for me, and I felt like I didn't have a friend in the world. It must have really shown, because Chuck came up to me after a class and asked me if everything was okay and if we could talk."

"Here was the most popular athlete in our class, noticing me, a nobody.

"We met right after school and talked for a short time, where he told me about Jesus and how much He loves me. We couldn't talk long since I had to get home and Chuck had football practice. But he gave me a small flyer, which he called a tract, that told me more about Jesus and how I could know Him.

"As soon as I got home, I read through the flyer several times. It told me things that seemed too good to be true. But I decided to trust what it was saying, and I prayed the prayer that was as the end of the flyer. I don't know what all happened, but the moment I did,

I felt free, like a huge weight had been taken off my shoulders and my heart was clean."

"I couldn't wait to tell Chuck the next day."

The extent of Chuck's witnessing was seen in the response that occurred at Chuck's funeral. After several people shared memories and antidotes about Chuck, and after Mike Mecurio had spoken on behalf of TTLC, Pastor Gaskell brought a very clear presentation of the gospel.

As he finished, he said, "What Chuck had that made him special is something that is available to every one of you: a personal relationship with God through faith in Jesus Christ as his Savior. I invite you to do what Chuck did several years ago and reach out in faith and receive Jesus as your Savior. I am not going to give an altar call at this time because I don't want you to make a knee-jerk decision based on the emotions of this moment. I want you to make a conscious, deliberate decision with your mind as well as your heart to trust in Jesus alone for your salvation.

"If you want to know more about having this relationship with God that Chuck had, or if you are ready to receive Him now, see me after the service or call me at the church and we will get together and talk."

In the following two weeks, Pastor Gaskell met personally with twenty-eight people who received Jesus as their Savior! These twenty-eight people represented a cross-section of Chuck's life—classmates, neighbors, teachers, coaches, and school administrators—all people to whom Chuck had personally witnessed. Again and again, Pastor Gaskell had people tell him, "I don't know what it was that Chuck had, all I know is that it is missing in my life, and I want it!"

In the days following Chuck's funeral, his classmates wanted to show their love and respect for him. Spontaneously, classmates began to collect money in honor of Chuck. Before long, classmates of Chuck's would show up at the house with coffee cans full of money along with a simple explanation, "We wanted to do something to help remember and honor Chuck, so here ..." as they handed Uncle Bill or Aunt Mim the can of money. As word spread, larger donations began to arrive.

Chuck's parents didn't know what to do with this generous outpouring of love. They wrestled with how best to use it to remember Chuck's legacy. After consulting with school administrators, they decided to put all the donations in a special fund to be used for college scholarships for deserving students. The following spring, at what would have been Chuck's graduation, the first Chuck Schnittker Memorial Scholar-Athlete Scholarship was awarded to a senior athlete who had played on a varsity squad for at least two years while maintaining a B+ or higher grade point average throughout high school. This scholarship continued to be awarded to deserving seniors at Rich Central High School in Olympia Fields, Illinois, until 1991.

Tim also had a life-changing testimony. The following summer I had graduated from high school and was able to take a week off from working on my dad's farm to again be a sergeant at Trail to Life Camp during Senior Boys Week. One of Tim's brothers was in my squad that week.

One day, during free time, he and I were in our cabin, and I asked him to tell me more about Tim.

"Our dad had come to faith in Jesus several months before camp last year at a revival meeting at the nearby church," he began. "The change in him was so dramatic that it was scary at first. He was different in every way. He kept telling us that we needed to come to Jesus, but none of us had.

"But then Tim came to camp and became a follower of Jesus. When he came home, he wouldn't shut up about Jesus. He kept telling us about how Jesus loved us and how we could know Him personally. Suddenly, what Tim was saying, as well as the change in my dad, made sense. So one evening, he prayed with me and led me to faith in Jesus.

"What is also cool, is that just before he left for Canada, Tim led one of our sisters to Christ."

Tim's brother went on to tell me that in the year since Tim's death, as far as he knew, his entire family had come to saving faith in Christ: all his siblings, mom, grandparents, aunts, uncles, and cousins! Tim was the catalyst for what has become a godly, Christ-centered heritage for the Meadows family. All this happened because one teenage boy said yes to surrendering his life to Jesus and then told other people about it.

The only knowledge of the Bible Tim had was the little bit he had picked up by attending church as a non-believer for a few months and what he learned at TTLC in one week of camp. He was still a spiritual infant, yet he had the presence and power of God in His life, and that was all he needed as he told people about how he received the gift of eternal life. As a result, he brought the message of salvation to people who mattered most to him, and three generations of the Meadows family were transformed for eternity.

As I watched the powerful impact of these three young men's lives unfold over the years, I realized something about my life. If I had drowned that day, there would have only been flowers, tears, and a lot of sad people at my funeral. There would have been no rejoicing in heaven over people coming to faith in Jesus because of my witness.

In other words, I had wasted much of the first seventeen years of my life. Though I knew Jesus as my Savior, was active in church, and even strove to read my Bible and pray every day, I had in many ways relegated Jesus to the back seat of my life. I had allowed my relationship with Jesus to slip into a religion with a lot of dos and don'ts, with very little power or impact on my daily life.

Though I had never made a conscious decision to do so, the choices I made every day showed that I had simply added Jesus to my life instead of surrendering it to Him. He was more of a consultant to me than Lord. My goals and desires were my priority, and I allowed

Him input when I felt I needed it. I was fulfilling my will, not His. As a result, I was doing very little that bore any eternal fruit.

That day when I sat on the rock set me on the path that was going to change all of that.

Looking back, I now realize that the commitment I made that day to surrender my life to Jesus marked the point when I started to fall in love with Jesus. I had known that Jesus loved me with an unconditional love, but then I started to truly love Him back—not because I had to or because it was expected of me but simply because I wanted to love Him and know Him on a much deeper level.

Obeying Him no longer came from of a sense of obligation or guilt; now it came as a privilege. I had the awesome honor of serving the King of Kings and Lord of Lords out of love. Any acts of obedience were just tangible expressions of my love for Him.

Don, Chuck, and Tim had this kind of love for Jesus, and they left strong spiritual legacies behind. Legacies that continue to impact lives decades after their deaths. Their lives truly made a difference.

Through the years I have crossed paths with of a number of the guys that were on the canoe trip with me. It is exciting to see how many of them are pastors, missionaries, Christian school and college teachers. Others have had effective ministries serving the Lord working as truck drivers, carpenters, businessmen, engineers, firemen, police officers, or serving in the military. I wonder now if each one must have sensed God's calling on his life that day on Opeongo Lake.

For Uncle Bill and Aunt Mim, the call on their lives was dramatic. As they talked and reminisced with others about Chuck as part of their grieving process, they openly shared what it was that had made Chuck's life so special—the Lord Jesus. As they did, people came to saving faith in Christ.

To help get these new converts grounded in the Word, Uncle Bill and Aunt Mim started Bible studies in their home. Soon their home became a center for ministry in their community as they reached out in their everyday lives and shared the sweet love of Jesus—whether it was helping a neighbor find a job or offering support when one of them experienced a tragedy.

They noticed that there were a lot of kids wandering around with nothing to do, so Uncle Bill and Aunt Mim recruited them into an ice cream bar and popsicle business. They outfitted the kids' bicycles with ice coolers packed with ice cream novelties and cooled with dry ice, and sent them on routes throughout the neighborhood to sell them. Not only did this give the kids a source of income and instill a work ethic in them, but it also opened many doors to witness to them. Even as their neighborhood began to deteriorate outwardly, the Schnittker house remained a lighthouse for the gospel.

That all changed in 1980.

One day Uncle Bill came home early from work and announced, "I've been fired! The insurance company at work instituted a new policy and mandated everyone who exceeds an arbitrary number of points on their driving record will no longer be insured. So they had to let me go."

After spending some time talking it through with the Lord, Uncle Bill and Aunt Mim felt He was giving them an opportunity to fulfill a long-time dream to move to Arizona. All their kids were grown and out of the house except Jan, who was completing her college education. The only thing standing in their way was the sale of their home.

Real estate in their neighborhood was dead. There were already eleven houses for sale on their street alone, and some had been on the market for over two years. Undeterred, they called a real estate agent they knew and met with her at 8:30 the next morning to list their house. At 4:00 p.m. that same day, they were again sitting at their kitchen table with the real estate agent, this time signing papers and accepting a purchase offer on their home! The Lord sold their house in less than eight hours!

About a month later, with an Airstream trailer hooked to the back of their car, they left on what was supposed to be a three-month trip through New York, North Carolina, Florida, and Texas to visit family and friends on their way to Arizona where a new job and partial retirement awaited. However, the Lord had different plans.

As they arrived at the Jungle Aviation And Radio Service Center (J.A.A.R.S.), the technical support arm of the Wycliffe Bible Translators based in Waxhaw, North Carolina, one of the friends they were stopping to visit was walking out of the administration building with other members of the management team.

"Bill and Mim!" their friend exclaimed when he saw them. "I can't believe the timing of your arrival. You could just be the answer to our prayers!"

"Hey guys," their friend called out to the other people with him, "I want you to meet someone."

The next thing Bill and Mim knew, they were learning of the immediate need for a food service director at the center. The management team was just coming out of a prayer meeting where they had asked the Lord to send them someone immediately to fill this important vacancy. And there stood Uncle Bill and Aunt Mim.

An impromptu job interview took place on the spot, and Uncle Bill and Aunt Mim were asked to prayerfully consider accepting the position on a temporary basis. They went to their guesthouse and prayed late into the night about it.

When they awoke the next morning, Aunt Mim climbed out of bed first and saw a sunbeam shining through the window and illuminating one specific verse on her Bible that lay open on the dresser—Isaiah 40:31: "But they that wait upon the LORD shall renew their strength; they shall mount up with wings as eagles; they shall run, and not be weary; and they shall walk, and not faint" (KJV).

They both felt that this was the Lord's confirmation that they should take the position. It was apparent to them that they were not to continue to pursue early, partial retirement. The Lord still had work for them to do. As a result, they accepted the temporary position and started immediately.

The longer they worked there, the more they fell in love with the ministry of J.A.A.R.S. and Wycliffe Bible Translators. Soon they realized that the Lord was calling them into full-time ministry as official missionaries with Wycliffe Bible Translators. When most people are starting to enter retirement, Uncle Bill and Aunt Mim stepped out in faith and began an adventure in ministry that they never dreamed was possible. It was an adventure that took them to Calgary, Alberta, Canada and later to Catalina, Arizona (outside Tucson), as Translation Center Managers, coordinating the physical support network for the Bible translators working with the indigenous tribes in those areas.

It was clear that when Chuck died, Uncle Bill and Aunt Mim picked up the mantle of ministry. They faithfully served the Lord until the day they too entered the starting lineup in heaven. Uncle Bill died of a heart attack in 1997 and Aunt Mim died in her sleep in 2001.

> "Precious in the sight of the LORD is the death of his saints." (Psalm 116:15)

> "Well done, good and faithful servant. You have been faithful over a little; I will set you over much. Enter into the joy of your master." (Matthew 25:21)

CHAPTER FIFTEEN

MORE THAN A PILE
OF ROCKS

It was July 22, 1970—two days after the tragedy on Opeongo Lake.

As the cars pulled into the driveway of Trail to Life Camp, our trip home from Algonquin Provincial Park came to an end, and I found myself wrestling with a strange desire: I wanted to go canoeing.

But wasn't canoeing the cause of my friends' deaths? Wasn't canoeing the cause of my own near-death experience? Wasn't it canoeing that had thrown countless people into a cauldron of grief and sorrow by ripping gaping holes in three families?

So why did I feel a compulsion to climb back into a canoe and pick up a paddle? It didn't seem to make sense, but I couldn't shake the feeling that canoeing was exactly what I needed to do.

As our cars came to a stop in front of the mess hall, a crowd of worried parents, family members, friends, TTLC staff, area pastors—as well as inquisitive newspaper reporters and photographers—enveloped us. As we stepped from our cars, we were greeted with hugs and tears and countless voices saying, "I'm so sorry."

We all gathered in a huge circle in front of the mess hall, held hands, and prayed. There must have been sixty to seventy people in the circle, while the reporters and photographers chose to stand outside the circle, watching. It was a precious time of talking with our heavenly Father. Person after person prayed and poured their hearts out to the Lord. Young and old, family members and strangers, we were joined together as the body of Christ. Together we were comforted by "the God of all comfort" (2 Corinthians 1:3). After a while the prayers subsided and a leader closed in prayer.

When the prayer time ended, a number of small groups formed around various survivors and listened to our accounts of the accident. Some found themselves being interviewed by the newspaper reporters. Vernon and I talked with several people we knew as we gathered our gear and dumped it into the trunk of my car, but I wasn't ready to go.

There was something I had to do.

Walking to the headquarters building, Vernon and I grabbed canoe paddles and lifejackets and made our way to the lake. Several other guys joined us in climbing quietly into several canoes and putting out on to the water. The water was as smooth as glass, and the muffled voices of those still milling around by the cars faded into silence as we paddled away from shore.

Little was said as we randomly paddled around the lake. A reverent quiet and sense of awe seemed to settle on the water. As we glided over the water, a flood of memories filled my mind—the smile on Don's face when another squad mate and I won the canoe race for our squad my first year at camp, the crazy times we had at the swimming hole, all the times Chuck and I competed against each other on the obstacle course, and the scene at the small fire pit between the lake and the obstacle course where just a couple of weeks earlier I had been inducted as a Man of the Star.

This was much more than climbing back onto the proverbial horse after falling off. It was an acknowledgment that the Lord had not deserted us and that He was still at work. We were numb with shock and needed a tangible reminder of His presence as well as the assurance that He was going to help us face the coming days.

Somehow that quiet time in the canoe provided it for me—it seemed to connect my past with the reality of the present, giving me a rock to stand on as I faced a storm of grief.

This was the beginning of my pile of rocks: my stones of remembrance.

Several times in the Old Testament, when people had a dramatic encounter with God or made a covenant with others, they would set up a stone pillar or make a pile of rocks that served as a tangible reminder of what had occurred at that spot. But these stones of remembrance also proclaimed a message. Strangers who asked about the significance of the rocks were told the story of what had happened there. This served as a guard against people forgetting the important lesson for which the stones stood in silent testament.

For example, when the Israelites crossed the Jordan River on dry land after God had miraculously temporarily stopped the flow of the river during the harvest floods, God instructed Joshua to build a simple memorial as a reminder of that great day. One man from each of the twelve tribes was chosen to go and pick up one large rock from the area where the priests who carried the ark of the covenant had stood in the riverbed. The story is recorded in Joshua 4:20–24:

> And those twelve stones, which they took out of the Jordan, Joshua set up at Gilgal. And he said to the people of Israel, "When your children ask their fathers in times to come, 'What do these stones mean?' then you shall let your children know, 'Israel passed over this Jordan on dry ground.' For the LORD your God dried up the waters of the Jordan for you until you passed over, as the LORD your God did to the Red Sea, which he dried up for us until we passed over, so that all the peoples of the earth may know

that the hand of the LORD is mighty, that you may fear the
LORD your God forever.

One thing the Israelites had demonstrated while on their journey
to the Promised Land was that they had very bad memories. God
miraculously rescued them from Egypt, brought them through the
Red Sea on dry land, provided food and water for them daily, made
his literal presence known to them on Mount Sinai, and protected
them from their enemies. How did they respond? They forgot. As
soon as something didn't go the way they wanted, they forgot the
miracles of God and turned away from Him.

I have come to realize how much like the Israelites I am. When
face to face with God answering my prayer or intervening in my life
in a dramatic way, I am quick to tell others about it and sing and
shout praise to the Lord. But let me go through some days when
things aren't going my way, and I get discouraged—even depressed.
I begin to wonder where God is, and I allow worry, anxiety, and fear
to move in. This is why I need a pile of rocks in my life to serve as a
tangible reminder of the goodness and faithfulness of God.

The Lord's intervention in every aspect of the canoeing accident
was miraculous, and on the day we returned to TTLC, I needed
to remember that. He truly was working "all things ... together
for good" (Romans 8:28). I could not risk forgetting what He had
already done for me or how He was still working in me. That is why
He led me to canoe around the lake at Trail to Life Camp—the lake
where Don taught me the basic skills of canoeing the first year I
attended camp.

I needed to remember that because God is on His throne, things
never go wrong; they only go different. I needed to remember that
when the headwinds of life relentlessly howl in my face, I can overcome them by exhibiting stug and paddling on. I needed to remember that when everything seemed hopeless, the Lord met me at the
bottom of the lake and lifted me up, enabling me to stand on a rock.

I needed to remember that He is God and He knows what He is doing—regardless of my inability to understand it completely. I needed to remember why God allowed me to be a survivor.

My pile of rocks turned out to be a passion for canoeing. I met with God on a level I never imagined was possible that day on Opeongo Lake, and as I paddled around the lake at TTLC, it was a time to "be still, and know that I am God" (Psalm 46:10).

Since that day, every time I kneel in a canoe and feel the grip and shaft of the paddle in my hand, I know I have come to my rocks of remembrance. It doesn't matter if I am paddling solo up a river or out on Lake Erie or Lake Michigan I remember. I can be paddling down a wilderness river in Canada with one or two other people in my canoe and come upon a bull moose—I remember. In the middle of winter with a snowstorm raging outside, I walk into my garage and hold my paddle in my hand and look up at my canoe suspended from the garage ceiling, and I remember.

In 1996 another stone was added to my pile of rocks. Bob Scodova and I took a trip to the North Arm of Opeongo Lake and camped near the site of the accident. Before we made camp, we spent time intentionally paddling through the events of the accident, visualizing and talking about what happened when and where.

"We were right here when we heard the cries for help from Chuck, Vernon, and Dan," I exclaimed, as I looked over my shoulder and suddenly flashed back to 1970.

I was in the stern, so I turned our canoe and paddled to the spot I remembered, and from there we worked our way through the events of that day.

"Duane, you were about here when your canoe went down, weren't you?" Bob asked.

I shivered as a chill came over me. "You're right," I answered.

A few minutes later, we were paddling toward the shore when suddenly I realized we were over the spot where Don, Chuck, and

Tim drowned. How I knew that, I'm not sure—it's not that there were any landmarks or markers on the water to identify the spot.

I just knew.

"Bob, stop paddling," I said. "It was right here that Don's canoe went down and the guys died."

We sat there silent for a few moments, and then Bob spoke, "Why? Why did they have to die? I can't shake that question, Duane. My heart still breaks every time I think of them."

"I wish I knew, Bob. I wish I knew," I replied. "But I know now more than ever that the Lord is still using all that happened here for His glory. Some day, when we are in His presence, we will be able to comprehend the big picture."

"One thing that I do know," I continued, "as I have relived that day in my mind a million times—the Lord was with us through it all. Just as He promised, He never left us, nor abandoned us. In fact, He was in us and in Don, Chuck, and Tim, just as His Word promised: 'Christ in you, the hope of glory'" (Colossians 1:27).

After a few minutes, we paddled to shore, to the big rock where we had climbed out of the water. We were surprised to find that the area where we had pitched our tent and built the fire had been kept clear through the years. It was evident that someone had cut several trees down, and the circle of stones that Jerry had put together as our fire pit was still there!

As heart-wrenching as the whole experience was for both of us, it was something that was long overdue. It helped bring closure in our hearts and souls.

That evening, as I watched a beautiful sunset over the area where the accident had taken place, I sensed the Lord's presence. A gentle breeze was blowing off the lake, and several nearby loons were singing their haunting song. As I sat there lost in the beauty and peace of the moment, I found myself praying, "Lord, thank you that this wasn't an accident in your eyes. I continue to trust you and I want to keep serving you. I want to someday hear you say, 'Well done, good and faithful servant.'"

❋

The purpose of having stones of remembrance is twofold: in addition to serving as a tangible reminder, stones of remembrance provide opportunities to tell others of the mighty works of God in our lives. Joshua made that clear when he set up the rocks at Gilgal. "When your children ask their fathers in times to come, 'What do these stones mean?' then you shall let your children know ..." (Joshua 4:21–22).

Canoeing has provided me with countless opportunities to share the gospel through retelling the account of the canoeing accident and sharing how the Lord worked through it. My love for canoeing is so evident that people often ask why I have such a passion for it, and this opens the door for me to share my story with them. Canoeing opened my eyes to how much the Lord really loves me and has caused every fiber of my being to fall in love with Him. I want other people to know the same thing and to receive His gift of love by trusting in Jesus alone for their salvation.

In 1976 I led my first wilderness canoe trip in Algonquin Provincial Park. It was the first and only canoe trip Trail to Life Camp ever took back to Opeongo Lake after the accident. When we came into the North Arm of Opeongo Lake, we stopped at the small island. Bob Scodova, my assistant leader, and I then shared the account of the canoeing accident with our fellow canoers.

"You have all heard about the deaths of Don Enzor, Chuck Schnittker, and Tim Meadows. Well, right out there is where it all happened," I explained, pointing to the area that lay before us. "And over there is where those of us who survived came ashore," I said as I pointed to the spot on shore.

I went on to describe what had happened that day. Bob would

jump in with his perspective of all the turmoil and challenges we faced as we tag-teamed in retelling the story.

When I got to the part of the account where I climbed into the canoe, I remained true to my self-deception (this being before my seminary days confession) and said, "... and someone climbed into the canoe, forcing it down and out of everyone's reach."

After we finished describing the accident, Bob went on to share what happened when he and Wes Sperr paddled over to the island we were standing on to tell the rest of our group about the tragedy.

"As we paddled up to this spot, one of the guys grabbed our canoe to steady it, while we climbed out," Bob explained, as we followed him over to the spot where he had come ashore. "Everyone gathered around us, and Mike Mecurio kept asking, 'Is everyone okay?' I didn't say anything until I was standing in front of him, and then I quoted what Duane had said to me when Wes and I got back out to the accident site, 'Captain Don Enzor, Sergeant Chuck Schnittker, and Private Tim Meadows have all gone to be with the Lord.' Almost in unison came the cry, 'WHAT?' So I repeated exactly what I had said."

Bob and I continued to tell them about the miracles surrounding our rescue and other details of our ordeal. When we finished, I called out, "Okay, let's load up." As we paddled away from the island, no one said a word.

In a matter of minutes, we were canoeing across the very spot where it all happened. A holy hush surrounded us as we glided over that hallowed area of the lake.

That day that small island became a pile of rocks of remembrance for me. Since leading that first trip, I have led about two dozen canoe trips in Algonquin Provincial Park. Every time we canoe into the North Arm of Opeongo Lake, we stop at the island and I share my testimony of the canoeing accident.

Without fail, that is the turning point of the trip. Through the years I have seen a number of teenagers and young adults come to faith in Jesus Christ on these canoe trips. Again and again, I've had these new converts tell me that hearing this story and then canoeing across the very spot of the accident was what opened their eyes to their own mortality and their need for Jesus to be their Savior.

Everything that happened on July 21, 1970, appeared at the time to be a huge tragedy that caused indescribable pain and sorrow. And it was. Over the years, it is clear that Satan wanted nothing more than for harm and destruction to come from this tragedy. The truth is, though, that the Lord has turned it around and used for His glory—saving many people in its wake. God has transformed an area of Opeongo Lake from a place of tragedy to holy ground, creating a sacred place of worship and praise and a place of testimony to His power and mercy.

Ten years after the accident, I was again in Algonquin Provincial Park leading my youth group from Central Baptist Church in Trenton, New Jersey, on a wilderness canoe trip. It was the last night in the wilderness, and we were camped on the East Arm of Opeongo Lake.

It had been the kind of week that no one wanted to see come to an end. We had faced and persevered through all the challenges the trip had given us. We experienced the unimaginable beauty of the wilderness—forging deep friendships and an understanding of what it means to function as a team. We had done the loop of lakes that Trail to Life Camp had attempted in 1970, and now we had made camp for our last night in the bush. All we had facing us the next day was a twelve-mile paddle back to the southern end of Opeongo Lake.

As we sat around the campfire that evening laughing and goofing around, impromptu skits and good-natured kidding about memories from the week filled the air. We weren't going to let Diane forget about splitting her jeans and looking like a clown in the jeans she borrowed from one of the guys. After all, they were six inches too long and probably just as large around the waist. Fortunately, I had some extra rope she used to tie multiple belt loops together to help keep her pants up.

A pause in the activity prompted me to ask the group to share how the Lord had worked in their lives that week. One by one people began sharing their hearts:

"This trip has opened my eyes to who God is and how much He loves me," one of the teens who had prayed and received Jesus as his Savior that week began. "I can't wait to get home and tell my friends about Jesus."

One of the girls spoke up, "I really needed this week to get alone with the Lord to think and pray. There's a lot going on in my life right now, and I needed this time to work through it. I feel I have a sense of what God wants me to do when I get home."

"Man, Duane, I haven't been able to shake what you told us that first day when we stopped on the small island and you told us about the accident," another boy shared. "It caused me to realize how serious this all is, and that I have been wasting my life by not surrendering to the Lord. I want you all to know that beginning right now, that is all going to change."

Powerful testimonies like these, interspersed with songs of praise to God, words of encouragement to each other, and times of quiet reflection continued on as teens and leaders alike openly and candidly testified to how the Lord was working in their lives.

Well over two hours later, activity began to wind down. The sun had set long before, and it was time to call it a night. After a time of prayer, we stood up and began milling around. Some remained around the fire, basking in the beauty of the moment, while others started toward their tents for the night.

I walked down to the beach to have a few moments of quiet with the Lord before heading to bed. Several others in our group joined me, and we stood in silence looking out over the water at one of the most spectacular sights I have ever seen. There was no moon, no clouds, and absolutely no breeze. As I stood on that beach, I felt as if I was standing at the edge of space gazing out at the universe. The water, smooth as glass, perfectly reflected the stars and created the ideal canoeing environment.

What I didn't expect was that it was also creating an opportunity to add another stone of remembrance to my pile of rocks.

Several of us grabbed our lifejackets and paddles then put out onto the water. We paddled out from shore a bit and then stopped and drifted.

I laid my paddle down and slipped off my seat and sat on the bottom of the canoe, leaning back against the seat to gaze at the stars. Everywhere I looked I saw stars. I felt like I was floating in outer space. The constellations perfectly reflected on the water's surface, and floating on the water gave me the sensation of weightlessness.

As I sat and attempted to take all this in, the peace of God's presence filled my heart, and I became overwhelmed by the realization that the God who simply spoke words to create all of this truly loves me. Here I am, at best, the tiniest of viruses on this speck of dust we call earth in the expanse of all of creation, yet He knows me personally and is active in my life. God loves me so much that He allowed His Son, Jesus, to die for my sins so my relationship with Him could be restored. All I had to do was reach out in faith and receive the gift of eternal life.

The vastness of God overwhelmed me that night. He is truly God, and regardless of what life might throw at me, I can rest in Him.

What I was looking at that night was not even a drop of water in the ocean of beauty, glory, majesty, perfection, and holiness of the place we call heaven. Nor did it do justice to the true awesomeness of being in the presence of Almighty God. That is the overwhelming and indescribable wonder of eternal reality for Don Enzor, Chuck Schnittker, and Tim Meadows.

It is the reality that awaits all of us who have reached out in faith and surrendered our lives to Jesus Christ. It is the reality I have my eyes focused on and the reality I look forward to entering one day.

Because of this reality, I know that I am more than just a survivor. As the Scriptures tell us, "in all these things we are more than conquerors through him who loved us" (Romans 8:37).

One thing I do: forgetting what lies behind and straining forward to what lies ahead, I press on toward the goal for the prize of the upward call of God in Christ Jesus.

PHILIPPIANS 3:13–14

A NEW JOURNEY

Don Enzor was right. God did do something amazing on that canoeing trip in 1970, but it was far beyond what anyone could have imagined. He took what we thought was going to be a memorable and fun trip and turned it into a life journey.

During this journey, God has shown himself to be faithful and true. The truth of Psalm 18:30 became a reality: "This God—his way is perfect; the word of the LORD proves true; he is a shield for all those who take refuge in him."

His power, love, sovereignty, and compassion have been demonstrated again and again. He has shown that He is a God who is active in every aspect of our lives. There is no problem, situation, or need that is too small or too big for Him. When we call out to God, He meets us wherever we are and works His transforming power in us, saving us and bringing hope, peace, and healing to our hearts.

Along the way, the Lord opened our eyes to realities that exist where the human eye cannot see. He expanded our outlook on life to include the eternal. From that perspective, it became clear that things don't go wrong; they only go different.

This has not been a journey into religion but rather a journey into a relationship with the God of the universe—a relationship made possible through the death, burial, and resurrection of Jesus Christ.

It is a journey that begins with Jesus, ends with Jesus, and is all about Jesus. Along the way, forgiveness of our sin, cleansing from guilt and shame, and the opportunity to begin to experience life the way God created us to live it is made possible—all because of the transforming power of Christ that is at work in all who receive the gift of eternal life through faith in Jesus.

If you are on this journey with me, you know what I am talking about. However, if not, then I invite you to join me by surrendering your life to God and receiving the gift of eternal life through faith in the death and resurrection of Jesus Christ. It is not an invitation to add Jesus to your belief system but rather to trust in Him alone for your salvation.

If you want to receive the gift of eternal life, it is easy to do. Simply talk with Jesus (pray) as you would anyone and tell Him what is on your heart. Tell Him that you want the gift of eternal life by believing in Him.

Receiving this gift of eternal life through faith in Jesus Christ is a life-transforming experience involving three biblical steps:

1. Admit to God in prayer that you are a sinner in need of a Savior and that your sins have separated you from Him.

   > For all have sinned and fall short of the glory of God. (Romans 3:23)

   > For the wages of sin is death, but the free gift of God is eternal life in Christ Jesus our Lord. (Romans 6:23)

2. Believe that Jesus Christ, who is fully God and fully man, died for your sins on the cross and rose from the grave. And recognize that He alone is the way to God.

   > But God shows his love for us in that while we were still sinners, Christ died for us. (Romans 5:8)

> Jesus said ... "I am the way, and the truth, and the life. No one comes to the Father except through me." (John 14:6)

3. In prayer, confess Jesus as your Savior and Lord. This means telling Him that you are sorry for your sins and that you want to turn from them. Tell Him that you want Him to be your Savior, and ask Him to forgive you of your sin.

> If you confess with your mouth that Jesus is Lord and believe in your heart that God raised him from the dead, you will be saved. For with the heart one believes and is justified, and with the mouth one confesses and is saved. (Romans 10:9–10)

Confessing Jesus as your Savior and Lord is another way of saying that you are trusting in Him alone for your salvation and surrendering your life to Him. There is no other way into a relationship with God except through faith in Jesus.

> And there is salvation in no one else, for there is no other name under heaven given among men by which we must be saved. (Acts 4:12)

> For by grace you have been saved through faith. And this is not your own doing; it is the gift of God, not a result of works, so that no one may boast. (Ephesians 2:8–9)

When you reach out and receive this gift of eternal life, amazing things happen to you, as explained in these verses:

> *You become a new creation.* "Therefore, if anyone is in Christ, he is a new creation. The old has passed away; behold, the new has come" (2 Corinthians 5:17).

> *You become a child of God.* "But to all who did receive him, who believed in his name, he gave the right to become children of God" (John 1:12).

You are promised God's presence. "I will never leave you nor forsake you" (Hebrews 13:5).

I cannot begin to fathom what the entire experience of the canoeing accident would have been like if I had not been in this relationship with Jesus. His presence is what enabled me to deal with all the ramifications of what happened and opened my eyes to the wonderful ways He was at work.

It is my prayer that you choose to embark on this same journey.

FREQUENTLY ASKED QUESTIONS

Over the years people have asked me many questions about what happened on Opeongo Lake that July day in 1970. Here are a few of the most frequently asked questions.

1. **Why was there only one lifejacket or ski belt in each canoe?**

   In 1970, Canadian law did not require lifejackets for each person in a canoe. Canoes are required to have enough floatation built into them that when fully submerged, will be able to keep the heads of six average-sized people above water. Therefore, our leaders decided we didn't need lifejackets.

2. **Why was everyone wearing hiking boots or work shoes in the canoes? Isn't that dangerous?**

   You're right, that was really stupid.

3. **Wasn't it against the law to allow someone to ride on top of the luggage in the back of a station wagon (as Tim Meadows did when the team was on the way to Canada)?**

   This was 1970. Seat belts were optional, available only in higher

priced cars or as an after-market add on. Shoulder harnesses were
yet to be developed and an air bag was a derogatory term for a
person who talked too much.

4. Weren't you in violation of Algonquin Park policies by camping where you did, which is not an authorized camping site— and by having food in bottles and cans?

No. The policies banning all glass bottles and non-reusable cans
in the interior of the park, as well as the establishment of desig-
nated campsites, were not implemented until several years later
to help prevent misuse of the park and protect the pristine nature
of the wilderness.

5. In chapter 3, you mentioned soaping the outside of your cooking pots. Why did you do that?

Covering the outside of a pot with a thin coating of soap before
placing them on the campfire prevents the soot from the fire from
becoming charred to the pot, making cleanup dramatically easier.

6. Is the outfitter who supplied the canoes still operating the concession on Opeongo Lake?

No. The Miglin brothers took over the Opeongo Access Point
Concession in 1977. In 1990, Algonquin Outfitters, who have
been in business since 1961, became the operators and continue
to this day. I have used their services in every trip I have led and
have found them to have exceptional equipment and service.

GLOSSARY OF CAMPING AND BOATING TERMS

bow: the front of a canoe.

canoe gunnels (gunwhale): the upper edge of a canoe.

canoe strokes

> **draw stroke**: performed by the bowman (front) or sternman (back).
>
> **bow stroke:** a basic forward stroke performed by the bowman.
>
> **sweep stroke:** a steering stroke used by bowman or sternman.
>
> **J-stroke:** the more complex stroke the sternman uses to keep the canoe going forward in a straight line.

lee side: the side of an island or peninsula that is protected from the wind.

portage: a term that literally means "to carry." It is used to describe both the act of carrying a canoe or backpacks from one point to another, and the name given to the trail between lakes or around rapids and waterfalls, on which we carry everything.

rain fly: the second layer of a tent; its purpose is to make the tent more rain resistant.

ski belt: a popular, non-certified floatation device popular during the 1960s and 1970s that amounted to a thick, dense foam rubber belt worn around the waist.

stern: the back of a canoe.

"stug": "guts" spelled backwards. It was the word our group invented to describe perseverance—having a never-give-up attitude.

swamped: a term that describes having a canoe fill completely full of water.

thwart: the brace across a canoe.

ACKNOWLEDGMENTS

I want to recognize and thank all those who had input in this book. The process of reconnecting with each individual after all these years is indescribable. A special thank you to Russell Enzor, Aaron Enzor, Al Schnittker, Sandy Schnittker, Paul Schnittker, Dirk Schnittker, Janet Schnittker Connon, Yvonne Sturgill-Patterson, and Pastor Ken Parker, plus the Trail to Life Camp gang that was part of the canoe trip in 1970 with whom I was able to make contact: Mike Mecurio, Bob Scodova, Jerry Kochheiser, Gary Kochheiser, Dan Barnhill, Eldon Grubb, Kim Graham, Terry Cooksey, Al DesChamps, and Vernon Miller. You each provided unique and much-needed details of the events of that day.

Through the process of writing this book, Nancy B. Kennedy has coached, encouraged, and guided me. Thank you for your kind and candid wisdom. Your professionalism and knowledge of the publishing process has been invaluable. It is clear why you have had the level of success as an author that you are experiencing.

I also want to thank Crystal Russell, who took on the daunting task of the initial editing of this book before I submitted it to possible publishers.

My wife, Molly, has been at my side every step of the way. She walked with me through the dark nights of grief and encouraged me as the Lord took me through the healing process. I am truly blessed to have such a loving, faithful, and godly wife as Molly.

NOTE TO THE READER

The publisher invites you to share your response to the message of this book by writing Discovery House, P.O. Box 3566, Grand Rapids, MI 49501, USA. For information about other Discovery House books, music, or DVDs, contact us at the same address or call 1-800-653-8333. Find us online at dhp.org or send e-mail to books@dhp.org.